MATTER 10

Editor: Angelina Ayers
Poetry editors: Jamie Coward, Bill Cooper, Suzannah Evans, Fay Musselwhite, Ruby Robinson, Kate Rutter, Noel Williams
Prose editors: Brigidin Crowther, Tricia Durdey, Nick Howard, Dean Lilleyman, Laura Wake, Louis Wood
Script editors: Kate Hainsworth, Russell Thomas
Children's fiction editors: Rosemary Badcoe, Noel Williams
Photographers: Beverley Green (pages 16, 22, 78, 108, 114/115)
myprivatetokyo.co.uk
Mary Musselwhite (pages 12, 36, 42, 50)
www.wix.com/marymusselwhite/photography
Artists: Sarah Darling (pages 34, 60, 62, 96, 106)
www.sarahdarlingart.co.uk
Steve Holmes (pages 54, 72)
steve_holm88@hotmail.com

Copyright of the work selected for inclusion remains with the individual authors

With special thanks to: Claire Hill and Glenn Thornley at Eleven Design, Professor Maurice Riordan, Margaret Drabble, Will Robinson for our website and Professor Steven Earnshaw

Published by Mews Press

Printed by Northend Creative
Print Solutions

All rights reserved. No part of this publication may be reproduced or transmitted, in any form or by any means, electronic or mechanical, including photocopying, recording or any information storage or retrieval system without prior permission.

ISBN 9781843873228

Contact: matteeditor@hotmail.co.uk
www.makingwritingmatter.co.uk

Contents

8	Foreword *Margaret Drabble*
13	BOULDER *Fay Musselwhite*
15	SLAM! *Daljit Nagra*
17	THE CONSTANT ART *Daljit Nagra*
18	AT THE BOTTOM OF CASTLE LANE *Dean Lilleyman*
20	BECAUSE *Dean Lilleyman*
23	FROM GHOST MILK: CALLING TIME ON THE GRAND PROJECT *Iain Sinclair*
35	HUMMINGBIRD *Angelina Ayers*
37	CADIZ *Angelina Ayers*
39	FIVE EXITS OFF A NARROW ROAD IN THE WOODS *Arto Vaun*
41	FATHER AND SON IN ORBIT (JULY 1969) *Arto Vaun*
43	FROM VIOLET *Laura Wake*
51	TOLLUND WOMAN *Rosemary Badcoe*
52	ELEMENTARY CATASTROPHE THEORY *Rosemary Badcoe*
55	YES! *Dean Lilleyman*
59	FALLING *Kate Rutter*
61	GRETEL'S NAIL *Kate Rutter*
63	QUEEN OF PUDDINGS *Tricia Durdey*
70	THE COXCOMB *Jamie Coward*
73	REMEMBER THE ALAMO *Diana Gabaldon*
79	FROM HOW TO KILL FRANCESCA. TWICE. *Noel Williams*
85	FROM MOTJIE'S SAMOOSAS *Tanya Chan-Sam*
97	RUT *Suzannah Evans*
99	FROM CAN LOBSTERS SWIM? *Elisabeth Von Aster*
107	THINGS I LEARNT IN JULY *Margaret Lewis*
109	DEJA VOUS *Lorna Festa*
118	*Alumni Talk Ten Years of Matter*
124	*Contributors*

Margaret Drabble
Foreword

There are many voices from many different places in this small volume, all of them speaking urgently to us in their distinctive accents. They are united by their connection with Sheffield Hallam, where creative writing has been encouraged to flourish for years, and some of them recognisably evoke the urban and suburban landscapes of Sheffield, and its surrounding countryside of millstone grit, heather and limestone. But others come from much further afield – from South Africa, America, India, the West Indies, Switzerland and from a distant planetary system of ice and fire. This multicultural polyphonic world glitters with imagination and bold endeavour, and takes the reader into newly invented territories.

The themes and genres are as varied as the voices. They range from the well-made short story, exemplified by Tricia Durdey's sinister *Queen of Puddings*, to the threatening but exhilarating drunken lower-case underworld of Dean Lilleyman's prose poems: from Lorna Festa's disconcerting exploration of decomposition and paranoia to Laura Wake's self-contained extract about a childhood experiment that goes wrong, convincingly narrated from a seven-year-old's point of view. Noel Williams's extract is from a humorous fantasy aimed at 12-year-olds, and is strikingly different from his work as a poet, some of which appeared in *New Writing Matter 9*. A radio play by Tanya Chan-Sam (who edited *Matter 8*) is set in drug-dealing Cape Town, and calls out for production, but is grimly lively on the page. It is encouraging to see such diversity, so much initiative.

It's usually easier to anthologise poems than prose, and poet and editor Angelina Ayers, along with her team, has made an impressive selection for Matter 10. Her own poems give us lyrical and sensuous glimpses of a warmer world, while Fay Musselwhite, Rosemary Badcoe, and others are more deeply rooted in a British or Nordic tradition. Kate Rutter's 'Gretel's Nail' is a chilling and powerful monologue, brilliantly reworking the Hansel and Gretel folk story. It packs into a few verses a wealth of wit and tragic insight, in a poem full of lasting resonance. 'Always hoping for something' is Hansel's judgement on Gretel, who 'could never believe in badness'. We do not know how this little narrative ends, but we can guess. Its imagery is shocking.

The guest writers reinforce the theme of geographic and linguistic diversity. Arto Vaun's poems come from a melancholy retrospective landscape of loss, Daljit Nagra's from today and tomorrow, forging a new language in a new typography. Diana Gabaldon's haunting story of the mission church at Alamo is a new look at a familiar legend, an evocative mix of topography and fantasy, where we cannot be sure what is fact and what is fiction. Iain Sinclair's contribution is a characteristically scholarly, informative, fantastic and personal essay in psychogeography, a genre in which all boundaries dissolve, and an inspiration to those writers who do not know which way to go, which journey to undertake. One of the many things that Sinclair's work says to us is: **be bold!** Take your own mental and literary journey, whether it takes you (as his did here) to Potsdam and Dublin and places in between, or whether it takes you back to your suburban childhood or onwards to outer space. Topography, as he says, is magical. You can create your own.

POETRY

Fay Musselwhite
Boulder

Only by bringing it home
could she get its measure.

How this was done
she doesn't remember.

She must have been drunk.
Now her favourite hunk of millstone grit

pulled from the river's bed
vested in moss and white oxalis

has swallowed the room
land-grabbed most of the carpet.

Her children inch round this cuckoo's egg,
listen to floorboards starting to give.

POETRY

Daljit Nagra
Slam!

       Pow to the Max
   to my West-Skin Brown-Side clarion call
 4 u East End Rajas & Ranis!   Go wake yor inna
    brown booty/yor Guru/
     How/How/Brown/How Brown/ Can u::::::::***Go!!!***//

I'm yor Gandhi at Zindabar Gate
                        drop yor jewels in the ring
come Mash up/Mash up
    their effffffffffffff'd up
        brown murdrin world
            enlightenin blaggerman wurd//

Can yoo heeaarrme?   **(BOO!)**
  I only suss yor   foundashun-nashun/
                  Vocalizashun/
            rhyme kondishun!

R u the poltroony Stooge// The Gang/Gang/Gangsta posa/
  who 'defecates on the microphone' with socially-political
           in:yor:face lines
          that are dressed as poems
         cos u kill to be a wordSMITH!

All u get is a talk-to-the-hand
from the Romo-Greeko smartarse bumchums

    them twee, 'propa'
    (yawn...yawn) Oxbrij
    P O W I T S!!!

POETRY

Daljit Nagra
The Constant Art

It's true my love's a paid up fashion victim.

Her hair, for a start, each morn is blandly ironed
glossy down her back; her nails are on nails
(embedded with gems) though when in heated kiss
they'll sometimes stay there hanging in my neck.

Yet she's no bendu dumbo reared on farms
to wrestle bulls, her battle's with tash and arms
she'll wax; but when I see her cut by friends
for wearing last year's cut, I think of times
I've worn my heart on the sleeve and that's not cool.

O love, these things are forging fickle youth!

Let's drop our guard for goods that rarely lie,
monuments like sonnets that will age
their solid lines in us to save our face.

bendu – villager (pejorative)

POETRY

Dean Lilleyman
at the bottom of castle lane

  orange lamplights snaking uphill to the bend. rose cottage 1910 gate open. nip in – tip bottle up two fifties and a ten. soft down steady don't chink. put note back in neck saying no milk today. stop, look and listen. under a black belly of laburnum tree. number thirty-three: four blue tokens: *us*eless. thirty-one, ten bob and a dog barking: *go on*, quick up the road soft-shoe close to the wall. slow down, look normal, headlights on treetops so tie shoelace. let big d's taxi go down slow. gone. thinking how close tonight: rache bradwell's tits over bra behind bainbridge. twenty-five, twenty-three, nothing. and next week i'm going under and she'll let me i know. dun roamin: six bottles: *which one?* and there, right at the back, two quid ten get in and *chink* ... *stu*pid. soft-shoe gravel back out past stupid pot cherubs and *run*. up past the bend to the lamp-lit bench and stop, and look, and listen: motorway hum from beyond the estate and coal-black fields as a bat

  skit flickers this arc of orange-lit trees, remembering last mischief when we dangled that suicide body of tights and scrunched-up news from the crook of that streetlamp, letting it swing out from the trees to shit the passing traffic, then later, when we lifted that window in the blackened-brick church, did a pint-pot ouija below the feet of a dirty jesus:

  is there anybody there? ... like fuck

  so we lobbed big books of god at each other, gargle sang strongbow and pissed in the font. and from the castle gates now the town as quiet as corn, remembering when we jimmied that lock to the keep, ghost-hunting the grey lady up spiral steps into that murder room with no window, slow closing the coal-dark door, sitting quiet as corn in the coal-dark cold, our breath unbraiding back from unseen walls ... and nothing ... and in all my life i have never seen a ghost – except – when sometimes you talk about it, i might say i have.

POETRY

Dean Lilleyman
because

the house loomed black beyond the last lamp-post. because it stood three floors high on its own bricked-off hillock. because the taxi bhangra fades when someone says my name. because he steps out from the shadow of a brick-built bus-stop wearing studs that glint on his face. because he tells me to come inside he'll sort me. because inside is a long dim hallway, doors with numbers and a flight of orange-lit stairs. because his flat has two other blokes on a dirty sofa. because the fat one is familiar and the sleeping one not. because the man i rang from the pub says *how much?* i say *an ounce*. because the fat bloke smirks i say *what?* he says *nothing*. because the man goes into a dirty kitchen, puts half a soap-bar into a dirty microwave, ping. because he says fifty, gives me a warm brown block that fits in my palm, then my pocket. because he grins and glints says *want to put some in a mix?* because i take my gear out, give it back to him with the money. because he passes it to smirking fatso. because fatso unwraps it, flicks a lighter to it, flame licking a corner. because i want to watch how much he crumbs off but can't. because the bloke i rang from the pub waves a freezer-bag half-full of pills in my face says *500 of the fuckers!* because he grins and glints says *want one?* because i say *yeh*. because i've not done them before i say i have. because i swallow it, take another. because fatso passes a bottomless plastic bottle curling with white smoke like spunk in a bath. because i nearly cough my ring up. because i tell them to put some different music on. because *this is shit.* because fatso laughs i say *what?* he says *nothing.* because i need water. because i think i'm going to chuck up. because back from the bathroom my face is drip wet with sweat. because the bloke i rang from the pub says *ten more for the pills.* because i've only got five he says *slate.* because i have to go now. because the door won't open. because when it does i fall through it. because the man picks me up says *that way don't forget.* because there are too many hallways and too many doors. because i fall down the last half of the stairs. because outside i find the road. because outside i find the moon. because outside i find home somehow, remembering trees and bus-stops and pubs, that i didn't get my gear back, that fatso's kids go to school with my kids, that next-door's koi-carp pond brings a river to my sleep, that eddies slow hush through a fern-filled gully, first light breaks white – through pine to a sway of open hand.

NON FICTION EXTRACT

Iain Sinclair
from Ghost Milk: Calling Time on the Grand Project

The Einstein Tower

Berlin's Olympic Park extended into hills covered with dense woodland, red roofs, white tower blocks, the domes of astronomical observatories. Smoke slanted from the chimneys of an energy plant on the banks of the Havel. We were back with the vision obscured by the wing of our descending aeroplane at Tegel, but now some of the shapes in the spread of the landscape have acquired meaning. After the Olympic showpiece in 1936, this park lent itself to demonstrations, military exercises. The stadium was a convenient space for rounding-up those who fell foul of the regime. In these woods, boy soldiers in the final insanity of the Third Reich were executed for desertion or cowardice.

   Spandau, at the edge of the park, is where Hitler's architect of ruins, Albert Speer, paced the prison yard for so many years. This dark-side apologist, who managed to smuggle out 20,000 scribbled sheets of warped testimony, is another proof that the critic Lotte Eisner was right when she said, 'Lang anticipated everything'. Words pouring from a caged superman, half-lunatic, half-sage: this is an accurate transcription of *Das Testament des Dr Mabuse*, a film made by Fritz Lang in 1933. And then suppressed by the Nazis. Rudolf Klein-Rogge plays a criminal mastermind, incarcerated in an asylum, controlling the city by telepathy, hypnotism and the production of endless pages of deranged script — which the authorities and their tame experts struggle to interpret.

At a time when the Situationists were denouncing each other and honing their provocations in Paris, Speer had already embarked on the ultimate psychogeographical exercise. Hitler's confidant marched in circles, following the shape of the noose he had so narrowly avoided. Round and round and round. He was flown to Spandau Prison in July 1947 and he remained there until October 1966: walking, walking, walking. He made meticulous calculations, he measured his stride and mapped the distance achieved on his self-inflicted treadmill against real-world geography. His first excursion carried him from Spandau to Heidelberg. Every hamlet along the way was visualised. He became the invisible spectre waiting to cross the autobahn. The ghost you think you see.

Muscles honed, destination achieved, the long-distance architect took on the world. Trenching the dust of the prison yard in summer, kicking aside fallen leaves, leaving footprints in the snow, Speer pushed on in the direction attempted by Céline and imagined by Francis Stuart, across Northern Germany, into Russia and Siberia. Crossing the frozen Bering Straits, he limped down the west coast of America, towards the proper destination for surrealists and psychogeographers: Mexico. By now he was the only inmate in this madhouse-prison. When they let him go, turning him loose into a twilight of self-justifying interviews, he was 35 kilometres south of Guadalajara. Starting there, I brooded, it should be possible to reverse the trek of this mental traveller, all those miles and years, back to Berlin. The demolished prison would then rise from the dirt and Speer's small plot of ground, the wilderness corner of the yard he called his 'Garden of Eden', would flower again. To reveal him as another premature ecologist.

On the last morning of our Berlin visit, we decided to adopt an excursionist mood, by taking the S-Bahn to the end of the line, to Potsdam. Here was the Filmpark Babelsberg, a Disneyfied reminder of the great days of Fritz Lang and the Ufa Studios, when Leytonstone's Alfred Hitchcock served his apprenticeship and witnessed the making of *Metropolis*. In Potsdam you could take your choice of palaces, museums, and memorials to conferences at which post-war Europe was carved up by the victors. We were pilgrims searching for a final structure to complete my triangulation: Fernsehturm, Bell Tower, Einstein Tower.

After the darkness of the tunnel, a canal and a splatter of graffiti on industrial buildings, we were soon among green places, botanical gardens, quiet suburbs, glimpses of white sails on water. A Chinese man stood beside me, so that his young daughter could take a seat. I remembered Christopher Isherwood's excursion to a villa at Wannsee. His host, the manager of a great Jewish department store in Berlin, describes his summer residence as an English 'country cottage'. But it is nothing of the kind: 'tame baroque, elegant and rather colourless'. The sort of villa acquired, at Am Grossen Wannsee 56-58, for the notorious conference convened by Reinhard Heydrich to fix the mundane technicalities of the 'final solution to the Jewish question'.

Touts come at you hard as you step from the train, offering bus trips and riverboat excursions. When I confess that my sole interest today is Erich Mendelsohn's Einsteinturm, they are happy to provide me with a map. Potsdam, from the station on, is a magical topography in which science fiction emerges from folk tale. And visionary architecture meets astrophysics in a forgotten crease of history. A green place smelling of pine-resin and good coffee.

The railway station, for some reason, is occupied by

lizard-headed extra-terrestrials, crouching Neanderthals, zipped apes and dinosaurs modelled in hard plastic. SMASH FASCISM! Walls at the bottom of the hill have been painted with cartoons of pylons in an electrical storm. Cock-rockets. And the red-purple skies of nuclear catastrophe. We are on the right track.

Through banks of golden sunflowers and modest well-kept houses, we turn into Telegrafenberg, a science park open to visitors. A woman, descending briskly, asks where we have come from. 'The station.' 'By which bus?' 'We walked.' '*You walked*, right from the station?' She is astonished and a little alarmed. It is unmannerly, she implies, to pass up the opportunity of experiencing the efficiency of public transport available in the capital of Brandenburg.

An occasional gardener is glimpsed, at a distance: this park is a silent world. One building, fronted with picnic tables at which nobody picnics, is the Polar Institute. The Institute of Astrophysics has a sympathetic connection with *Die Frau im Mond*, the film Fritz Lang made for Ufa from a script (based on her own novel) by his wife, Thea von Harbou. The surface of the moon was created in Babelsberg by importing truckloads of sand from the Baltic. The warp of space-time relativity is much in evidence. Equations laid out in Lang's speculative movie form the basis for Wernher von Braun's VI and VII calculations. East London is flattened by rockets rushed into production to publicise Lang's last silent film. Professor Hermann Oberth, who advised the monocled director on *Die Frau im Mond*, was frequently quoted by von Braun, at the period when he was responsible for research and development at Peenemünde. He liked Oberth's proposal for a spacecraft carrying a mirror, with a diameter of many kilometres, capable of concentrating the sun's rays to control terrestrial weather and manipulate hot spots.

The shifted dunes with which the texture of Lang's moon was constructed came from beaches near the secure site where von Braun and his associates were adapting fantasies of interplanetary travel into a technology for turning London into a lunar desert of craters and rubble. Chris Petit told me that when the Russians arrived in Potsdam, they occupied the Babelsberg studios, dressing themselves in costumes from a Napoleonic epic and driving their cattle through the sets of palaces and plywood cities. Terrified Potsdam inhabitants, primed by propaganda from Goebbels, were ready to believe anything, even Cossacks with shaggy ponies and camels. They accepted the latest invaders as a regiment of Frenchmen from 1815, returned from their battlefield graves to avenge the deeds of the Prussians at Waterloo.

On sandy paths, among the woods of Telegrafenberg, we are the aliens. I'm dressed in the sort of fisherman's many-pocketed waistcoat associated with Joseph Beuys. To be strolling here, pleasant as it is, so far from Hackney, is as eccentric as the solitary marches of Samuel Beckett in Tiergarten, or the nocturnal ramblings of Francis Stuart, both of whom espoused a sort of cultural relativism: curving movements through time and space, attempting to bring into focus their point of origin. Ireland is experienced most vividly when furthest away. And Dublin, that fabled walkers' city, with its long crescent bay, is grooved into the memory by pilgrimages through other countries, where equivalents are found for every bar and bench. Phoenix Park dissolving into Tiergarten, Ballsbridge into Charlottenberg. Goethe into Yeats.

Even the contemporary boom town, spreading up the coast like Los Angeles, a cancer of failed developments and ghost estates, had a defining image for me: young women, early in the morning, smartly presented, clicking down Baggot Street, into the Georgian squares with their polished brass plates, carrying trays from which polystyrene coffee beakers depend like udders. As if, in a flash, milkmaids had become independent women of the city. The same grand squares with their trumpeted literary associations were active in the holy hour of old, when the pubs would shut for a post-lunch lull, now with up-market prostitutes, economic migrants servicing the business community, the corporate drones who could not afford to take time away from their laptops. That business briskly dealt with before a late return to Sandycove, Dalkey or Beckett's Foxrock.

In a Telegrafenberg clearing, we came across a group of abandoned tin huts, so haunting and bizarre that I had to photograph them. Like a Viking settlement of upturned boats constructed from overlapping sheets of corrugated iron. Rusted skirts and a massive padlocked door. A hangar for some sinister experiment worthy of Dr Mabuse. An exercise in mind control. I thought of a report by Francis Stuart. After walking for many miles, struggling to make sense of Berlin, he strains for a solid metaphor taken from his native Ireland: the iron hut.

'He continued his walk which was not, after all, the exploration of a tourist but in the nature of a pre-pilgrimage to places, at present unhallowed, which might become as haunted for him as, say, certain corners of Dublin or the row of iron huts on the Curragh plain. How little he foresaw that nothing from the past had prepared him for what was to come!'

Erich Mendelsohn's Einsteinturm was suddenly there, of its time and our time: magnificent. It was the realised portrait of an idea: deep steps, recessed windows, an unashamedly priapic form. A sketch, swift and sure, manifested in the world, creating a force-field powerful enough to keep witnesses at a respectful distance. The tower grew out of a lawn, set among the woods, like the periscope of a submarine emerging from the earth. The thrust of a shamanic observatory from an era of discontinued modernism. Concrete maturing into radiant white skin.

A note was pinned to the door: 'Dear Visitors – The Einsteinturm is no museum but a Solar Observatory of the Astrophysical Institute of Potsdam.' We had walked, therefore, beyond the city of museums, beyond towers that were open to the public, sanctioned sites where tourists are invited to gaze in wonder at the achievements of past generations of men. In progressing around the meandering paths of the hill, we had triggered a more complex narrative, which would somehow play itself out against the shape of this expressionist structure.

The visionary homage to Einstein belonged in the film studios, down below us, with the wild-eyed scientists and mesmerists of Fritz Lang and Robert Wiene. In 1923, a year of hyperinflation in Germany, when loaves of bread cost 428 billion marks, Lang's scientific adviser, Hermann Oberth, published a 92-page book called *Die Rakete zu den Planetenräumen (The Rocket into Interplanetary Space)*. Inspired by his childhood reading of Jules Verne, Oberth – who lived, like Hitler, in Munich – contrived a text to fascinate filmmakers, as well as industrialists and ambitious students of engineering like Wernher von Braun. 'Interest in spaceflight often seemed to coincide with flight into hard-right politics,' wrote Wayne Biddle in *The Dark Side of the Moon*.

The Einsteinturm, built to prove the validity of the Theory of Relativity, worked in ways far beyond its original remit. Mendelsohn described it as a 'heavenly project'. The authorities in Potsdam dragged their feet over budgets and technical specifications, delaying completion to the point where the tower became operational at the very moment when Oberth's book was published. The white stump on its solid base was a launch pad for pure research. Equations formulated here were as dangerous in their implications as the Peenemünde rocket experiments that curved towards urban devastation, astral policing and dreams of total war.

Beautifully redundant from the start, Einstein's thesis having been tested and proved elsewhere, Mendelsohn's tower became an occupied sculpture conceived by a Jewish architect to honour a Jewish scientist: as well as a demonstration of the technological heritage of the defeated Reich. In its present form, after extensive restoration in 1999, the declared aim of the tower is: 'to gather data on solar and nuclear physics'. While its covert purpose, I discovered, was to shred received notions and dissolve them into the cosmic stew, a general theory of everything: physics and poetry, Dublin and Berlin. Celtic myths and the dark gods of the forest intertwined like vegetative script from *The Book of Kells*.

The physicist Erwin Schrödinger, who generalised Einstein's relativity by using four-dimensional geometry with anti-symmetric components and connections, received a personal invitation from Éamon de Valera to move to Ireland to help establish an Institute for Advance Studies in Clontarf. Appointed as Director of the School of Theoretical Physics in 1940, Schrödinger stayed in Dublin for 17 years, fathering two children after involvements with students, and becoming a devotee of the Vedanta philosophy of Hinduism. Individual consciousness, he believed, was only a manifestation of a unitary consciousness pervading the universe. He apologised to Einstein for recanting on his outspoken criticism of the Nazis, a position he was forced to adopt in order to safeguard his tenure at the University of Graz. It was in correspondence with Einstein that he proposed the thought experiment in which a cat is neither alive nor dead. Or both at the same time.

Affected by the vision of the tower, I returned with Anna for a fortnight's stay in Dublin, the city in which we had met as students, but never revisited. Space-time anomalies permitted us, like Schrödinger's cat, to be in two places at once, and blessed with a special tenderness for the seatown in the rain, as we walked or re-walked half-remembered routes between Howth Head and Dalkey. Anna said that she had seen more in this brief stay than in the four years of her student life, which was now a kind of dream. A trio of old folk, out on the razzle, made it their business to find us the site of the vanished hotel where we spent the first night of our married life. In the long light evenings, possessed by an agenda of her own, Anna tracked down the bars that had survived and the ones that had transformed themselves into Mexican restaurants or tourist hotels. The priests had gone from the streets and the beggars were site-specific professionals from the Balkans. One night we took ourselves off to a travelling circus pitched alongside the house where Bram Stoker was born.

We had been on the move so long now that it was impossible to fix our coordinates. We slumped on a bench, in a damp park, or a windblown square in mid-construction, and the world raced past us. Potsdam on the S-Bahn was Shepperton out of Waterloo: green spaces, reservoirs, film studios, the connection to the city stretched to its limits. Hermann Oberth's proposal for the spacecraft with the giant mirror could have come straight from J.G. Ballard's *Vermilion Sands*. When the painter Brigid Marlin sent me back to *The Kindness of Women* in search of her fictionalised presence, I found an incident that could only happen when time was being sucked into a black hole. Ballard and Fritz Lang, two confirmed self-mythologisers, come face to face. And it happens in South America.

'An elderly man in an oversized tuxedo sat on a straightbacked chair turned sideways to the wall. He slumped in the chair like an abandoned ventriloquist's dummy, buffeted by the noise and music, the light show dappling his grey hair a vivid blue and green. He looked infinitely weary, and I thought that he might have died among these garish film people. When I shook his hand and briefly told him how much I admired his films, there was a flicker of response. An ironic gleam flitted through one eye, as if the director of *Metropolis* had realised that the dystopia he had visualised had come true in a way he had least expected.'

Iain Sinclair

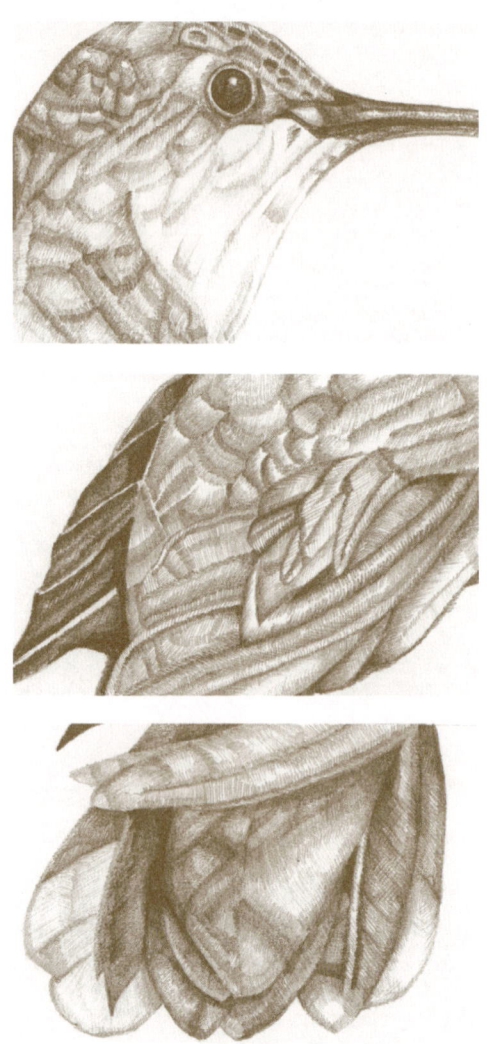

POETRY

Angelina Ayers
Hummingbird

See how the uncambered wings of a hummer
beat a hundred times a second
                                    to hold it still.
This flicker of greyed light is the half memory
of a ginger plant behind a beach

                thick stem clusters
                      cupping a small sunrise
              close by Dad's shed

corrugated rust and gunmetal blue
squinting into the early day.
                      He rubs his bare feet
on the sand-flecked floor, talks of England

how her green curves rise
                and fall like breath
and every home has its own icebox
and each son will have his own perishables.
He relights his pipe
                looks out to his ginger tree
   where the hummingbird hovers, whips all its energy
into this one trick of feeding mid air.

POETRY

Angelina Ayers
Cadiz

Spooning under a ripe-red serape
    a film of sweat between us
        we feel
                the curl of the sea
lift the hull
      of this old fishing boat, paint flaking
           our toes tangled in drift net.

The skyline is chipped pine and oarlock
      the green glow of a streetlamp.
Your ribs
      rise into my back
           and with each out-breath
    a new tale

      nomadic mouflon, gypsy tribes
      trekking over mountain tracks

the smell of charred grass and kindling
    shed like crumbs for us to trail.

You talk of the night Hannibal left for Rome
    his Iberian princess
           the way her black hair
froze as they crossed the Pyrenees.

POETRY

Arto Vaun
Five Exits Off a Narrow Road in the Woods

1.
Often do I think about gods who I know nothing of
My eyes shut and Sigur Ros and a din everywhere
It is embarrassing

2.
My dead are further and further away lately they seem
Like birds but never rest on my forearm for long
I reckon I know nothing of them as well

3.
How I want to shake down cowardice
To wander in the dark plains as a horse might
With the dense-boned posture of antiquity

4.
Yet I am but a panting man an unsure body
It matters not that the dust whipping about
Is from guts and stars from the ends of our very hair

5.
So I come to you with shards and letters
I come splintered and melodic yes
Like old songs crackling to themselves low

In the wet-skinned trees and tense houses

POETRY

Arto Vaun
Father and Son in Orbit
(July 1969)

- for Michael

I am done talking about the moon – its lit body
Does not caress, does not notice even the few
Footsteps being left there right now, weightless crushes
Upon its cold skin, its zero memory, austere
Imprints that will remain precise in their loneliness
Far, far past us, sitting here – father, son, static
On the television mimicking our locked insides

As audience, we are perfect – facing forward, speaking little
And well dressed, even for this, even in our own home
Your pale hands adorned with age spots, adorned
With a solidity and conviction I fear to comprehend
Just as perhaps you fear yourself randomly, alone in bed

A scratchy voice from the pathetic dark distance
Reaches our living room, falls to the floor from gravity

NOVEL EXTRACT

Laura Wake
from Violet

I am allowed to stay up late only when nature programmes are on. Tonight it is just me in the lounge as Dad is working in the garage and Mum is in bed. I watch a programme about vets and then it is a David Attenborough one who I like because he is brave enough to crawl into a termite nest. Tonight the programme is about the hazel dormouse who doesn't just hibernate in winter but sometimes just because there is not much food around. The programme says that the dormouse and the bat are the only animals in England who hibernate properly. The dormouse can live for months without moving at all. In the spring it comes out and starts running about in the trees and bushes eating acorns and berries. The branches are a bit like a high street with shops because it runs around on them like we walk on paths and chooses different foods as it goes along. If I was a dormouse I'd spend more time awake walking about in the trees. In one part of the programme a dormouse is eaten in one bite by an owl. It is really sad but I know that it is nature.

At the end of the programme nobody comes to tell me to go to bed so I decide to stay up. I watch a programme where a woman has a husband and a boyfriend. The husband comes home from work early and the boyfriend has to hide and then climb out of the window. He is only wearing some pants and looks funny. I watch the whole thing. There is a bit of swearing and in one bit a man in a bar throws a drink all over a woman's fur coat. I think she deserves it as it's cruel to wear fur. The news is on after and it's a bit boring and I start to feel tired.

I wake up and on the television is just a picture of a girl, a blackboard and a clown; there is also a tiny screaming sound. I turn it off and the noise stops. The house is completely dark and quiet. I run upstairs to bed.

When I get up I hear birds singing outside. Mum calls it 'The Dawn Chorus' but it is later than dawn and light outside. There are two blackbirds on the grass; one is pulling up a worm and the other is just hopping about. The one pulling up the worm is brown so I know it is the female. I go and brush my teeth then peek into Mum and Dad's room. Dad isn't there but Mum is still sleeping.

'I'm going to have breakfast,' I say. She doesn't say anything. I climb onto the bed; she is on her side and I lean over to ask her, 'Do you want some?'

She doesn't open her eyes but says, 'No thank you, Violet.'

I get up to leave and then she turns over fast and opens her eyes, 'Not too many Coco Pops ok.'

'I won't.'

My mum is a bit like a dormouse at the moment, but it's not that cold yet, and we always have food in the house. I open a brand new milk bottle even though there is one already open and pour it over my Coco Pops. The cream from the top of the milk sits on top of them and I will save it till last. Sometimes the birds get to the milk earlier than my dad and peck through and eat our cream. I eat my cereal and decide that today I am going to do a miracle.

When Benjamin comes round we usually play by the muddy swamp. The muddy swamp is at the very end of the garden behind the trees. When you are down there it is like being in a dark tunnel made of trees. The water is the colour of fire mixed with rust. If you look carefully you can see patches of rainbow-coloured swirls like on petrol station floors. The muddy swamp stinks. Mum and Dad talked about filling it in; Mum says it looks 'nuclear'. In the end they decided to leave it because of 'drainage'.

Benjamin is frightened.

'Go on,' I say. 'Jesus was just a normal person and he walked on water.'

'I don't know; what if it doesn't work?'

'Of course it works; you just have to believe. I did it this morning.'

'Can't you show me first?'

Benjamin's nose is always runny and he never wipes it. In one nostril is a bubble of snot.

'I can't show you. A miracle is something you have to make yourself do without any help. Once you've done it once though we'll both be able to do it together.'

'Really?'

'Yes. It'll be brilliant. We'll be able to run all the way down the muddy swamp to the sea.'

'Ok.'

As he climbs down closer to the edge he slips a little bit because his Wellington boots don't grip well.

'Go on!' I say. 'You can do it!'

He steps out onto the water and it works. I am sure he stands on top of the water; but then he goes through. I watch as he disappears completely. All that is left of him is a bubbling movement on top of the sludge.

I have to help him. I grab a stick and lie down on my tummy and poke at where he is. His head comes back up through the water. He looks like he is made of clay or chocolate; the orangey water has closed his eyes and nose. A hole opens where his mouth must be and he screams.

'I'll get help,' I shout but don't know if he can hear me and he goes under again and all I can see is his orange brown arms waving. I run up the garden as fast as I can. I have never had to call for help before.

'HELP!' I shout, 'HELP!' It is the weekend but I can't see

my dad anywhere. I run into the house shouting as loud as I can. Mum comes running down the stairs.

'What's wrong?'

'Benjamin's fallen in the ditch and can't get out.'

She doesn't say anything else to me but runs out of the house and into the garden. I can't keep up but run after her. She stops at the line of trees. She isn't wearing any shoes.

'Where? WHERE?'

I point to the place we enter the muddy swamp and she pushes through the trees. I don't need to show her where Benjamin has fallen in because one of his arms is sticking up through the water. My mum doesn't lie down like I did but jumps straight in. It can't be as deep as I thought because she can touch the bottom. She pulls him out of the water; he looks like a little orange doll; he looks like Morph on *Hartbeat*.

She keeps patting him on the back then she lays him down on the bank and opens his mouth. She pulls mud out with her fingers then she puts her fingers into his nose and takes the mud out of there too. I think I see his legs start to move.

'Go to the telephone, Violet, and dial 999, then ask for an ambulance.' I don't move. I am scared to ring 999.

'Now, Violet!' she shouts.

I run back to the house. I don't want to call 999. I almost start to cry.

The telephone is in the study on my dad's desk. I pick up the receiver and dial. I have always wanted to do this but now I don't. I know I will be in trouble.

A voice on the other end says, 'Emergency Services. Which service do you require?'

'An ambulance.'

'Is there an adult we can talk to?'

'No. My mum is looking after my friend. He fell in a ditch and I think he's drowned.'

'Ok, Sweetheart,' the voice says, 'do you know your address?'

I learned my address off by heart when I was five. 'Yes,' I answer and tell it.

It says, 'Tell your mum an ambulance is on the way.'

Mum has got our neighbours the Pearsons to come round. They are all in the drive with Benjamin and the ambulance. Mrs Pearson is German and has shouted at me before for trespassing in their garden. I told Mum and she said that Mrs Pearson is very protective of her plants and I should stay on our side of the garden. Mr Pearson's name is Peter.

The ambulance men put Benjamin on a little stretcher and lift him into the back. Everybody who has touched him has the orange mud from the muddy swamp on them. The ambulance men talk to my mum and say that they're doing something to his throat so he can breathe easier. The word sounds like tractor and honey. I ask to go in the ambulance but my mum says, 'No'.

She says, 'Mrs Pearson is going to stay with you until Dad comes home. I have to stay with Benjamin until his mum gets to the hospital.'

'Please can I come?'

'No, Violet.'

The ambulance men hurry her into the ambulance and the doors are shut behind her. She smiles at me but doesn't look happy as she waves goodbye.

Mrs Pearson puts a hand on my head and says, 'Come on, Violet, let's go and read one of your books.'

'Ok.'

It's not fair. I don't want to stay with German Mrs Pearson. Benjamin is my friend and I want to look after him too. It's not fair that my mum is looking after him either; she should be with me. I hope his mum gets to the hospital quickly and mine can come home.

Mrs Pearson and I take turns to read from *Nasty Tales for Nine Year Olds*. Even though I am only seven I have the whole set up to age 13. I choose a story about a boy who tries to steal an ogre's dinner. Mrs Pearson is brilliant at reading it especially the scary bits. She does a terrible booming voice for the ogre and yells, 'Verre ist my dinner, boy?' so loud that it scares me and then we both start laughing.

Dad comes home and tells me to wait in the kitchen while he talks to Mrs Pearson. They go outside to the drive. When he comes back he doesn't play with me or take me for a bike ride. He makes me sit down at the kitchen table and asks me lots of questions about Benjamin and the ditch. I don't want to tell him about the miracle.

'But why did he do it, Violet?'

'I don't know.'

'He wouldn't have just jumped in.'

'He didn't.'

'Well what happened then? Did you tell him to jump in?'

'He didn't jump, Dad.'

'Tell me the truth, Violet.' He looks me in the eye. He is holding one of my hands which I usually like but today it feels horrible and I wish he would let it go. If I tell a lie I will go to hell.

'I thought he would be able to walk on the water, Dad.'

He takes his hand away and lifts both his arms up in the air for a minute and then puts them back on the table.

'So you told him to do it.'

'Yes.'

My dad leaps up from the chair and makes me jump but then doesn't do anything. He turns and walks around in a little circle then goes to the sink and looks out of the window. We stay like this for a while. I wonder what the blackbirds are doing and if they have lunch like we do halfway through the day. I don't know if I am allowed to leave the table.

'Dad?'

He pours himself a glass of water and makes me a Ribena then comes and sits back at the table. He has forgotten to use my special cup but I don't say anything about it.

'Violet, you did a very stupid and dangerous thing today.'

I don't say anything but it wasn't a stupid thing I did.

'You are a clever girl, and I don't understand why you would do something like that. You know how water can be dangerous and you know that people can't walk on water which is why we have to learn to swim.'

'Jesus can,' I say.

My dad screws his face up and says, 'Jesus isn't a person, Violet; he's an angel. And anyway that doesn't matter. Benjamin is younger than you and you should be looking after him. He could have drowned today if your mum hadn't got him out.'

'He's ok now though isn't he?'

'No he's not. He's very ill and has to stay in hospital. You know how serious that is.'

'Yes, Dad.'

'Don't ever do something dangerous like that again.' And then he says loudly, 'Are you listening?'

'Sorry.'

'Promise me, Violet.'

I say, 'I promise.'

POETRY

Rosemary Badcoe
Tollund Woman

Six am: seclusion folds around me,
a winding-sheet, birds of memory trapped
and flapping inside my skin. I dance to Nerthus,
revel in the blaze of ergot. The grass runs,
dribbles down my arms, weaves greenness
into baskets. I empty beechnuts into them,
sharp cornered caltrops, answered antiphons.
Silent, I drink more tea: brown, green,
keen to preserve myself, acid as bog
bodies. I lie in peat, eat soup of bristlegrass
and gold of pleasure, tie a hide belt
around my waist, a garrotte around my neck.
My head tips back, detached. I fill with water,
feathered thumbprint stained upon the sky.

Rosemary Badcoe
Elementary Catastrophe Theory

Let us suppose that *a* is alone, at equilibrium,
making coffee perhaps, or gazing idly at the garden,
considering the hydrangea. Tiny perturbations
can reset parameters. Imagine a scenario
where *a* picks up the letter, lights a match,
drops the burning remnants in the fireplace.
Or envisage, instead, her reading, then regard the way
she wraps her arms around her, unexpectedly cold.
Observe while *a* hits zero, the tipping point:
things can go either way.

Let us now have *b* enter the equation, walk
down the path, ring the bell. We're on the cusp
of a catastrophe. Our stable outcome
can leap in an unexpected direction.
a opens the door, stares at *b*, but *b* is intractable,
his face shaded by the trailing clematis.
a does not know where she stands; vary *b*, and the system
oscillates, attracting and repelling.
She brings hand to mouth, remembers
sometimes the lilies, soft as fingertips, sometimes
the rough concrete grazing her face.

The future is unpredictable
where the exact state of a is unknown.
It may be that a will ponder past experience,
find it in herself to call the Alsatian to her side,
possess the gumption to slam the door.
One can consider what happens if b holds constant
and a vacillates. Observe a pitchfork bifurcation,
a choice of solution, neither of them good for a.
b will rip out the hydrangea, buy only herbal teabags,
chop down the clematis. a will exist only
as a derivative of b, a reflection, scraping thick mud
from her shoes, pockets full of seeds
she will never plant.

SHORT STORY

Dean Lilleyman
YES!

billy is having the best night of his life. everyone will love him, and his girlfriend anna will change her mind and let him finger her for sure.

life feels fucking great, billy's usual self-conscious restraints falling onto the pavement with each step, with each empty miniature gordon's gin cast under hedges, thrown into bus stops, back gardens, shop doorways, post-boxes, schoolyards, shopping trolleys, playgrounds, graveyards.

YES! billy is more alive than he has ever been, colours and movement, sound and sense, everything is different, better, new and improved. by the time the staggering billy reaches the church hall doorway he has already decided that this is how he wants to stay. forever. he smiles at the old lady who collects the entrance money, telling her how beautiful she looks.

love you, says billy with a nonchalant flick of the wrist, swinging back the dull thump-thump-thump doors to the sound of selector, that mod band that a headbanger like billy cannot dance to, cannot admit to liking amongst his headbanger friends, and yet, tonight, billy the incredible is crossing boundaries, squeezing the juice from the gonads of life, and jumping straight in amongst the trilby-headed, narrow-tied, two-tone knees-up of the bumboy mods.

YES! billy cries, pogoing dead-centre of the enemy, like a brick dropped into a bowl of milk, the ripple of astonishment stopping the running-on-the-spot suited dancers around the epicentre of billy.

WHAT THE FUCK YOU DOING? yells fat johnny into billy's ear as billy the wonderful lands from a deer-like spring through the air. billy fixes fat johnny with a bozz-eyed grin. *YES!* he shouts into fat johnny's face, but by now the modboys and beatgirls have all stopped their jag-kneed dancing to gawp. this will not do! but before they can decide on how to react to billy's crime of dance, the opening flourish of no more heroes by the stranglers causes a spiky tide of punks and punkettes to wash across the floor, studs and white paint on leather, tartan and straps and green-laced doc marts send the mods scattering to their corner of the church hall, and the grinning billy does the only thing he can do to celebrate this life, this wondrous gift of existence, and that is to do the twist.

and this, is where things take a turn towards the ugly: the punk boys and girls doing what they have to do too, which is to hurt billy in the form of dance, by hurling their pogoing spit and boot into the twisting, laughing fool that has the audacity not to dance the dance that has to be, stubbing their fags out in billy's face, which now hails a call to billy's headbanger friends, who up to now have been watching goggle-eyed and gob-smacked from their corner of the church hall, and can hesitate no longer as one of their own is kicked and spat on and used as an ashtray.

the music stops

and the elderly ladies and gentlemen of the church committee attempt to quell the push and the shove as best they can, and as the yellow light of fluorescence fills the hall, the white-haired reverend leads billy by the wrist to the fire-exit, the bloody-lipped three minute hero of the hour, grinning at the adoring crowd, knowing full well that he is now champion of the world, a new god, a name that will be passed from classmate to stranger, throughout the whole village to the town, billy, the boy who danced against the grain, the boy who everyone will want to be, want to be with, to fuck and to worship, the boy who started a revolution.

outside his bedroom window, the birds are singing to billy. billy wishes they'd shut up and leave him alone. he doesn't want to remember pissing his jeans at the top of the slide, standing open-armed and crucified like a pissy jesus, all the faces looking up and laughing as he tells everyone to piss themselves because it's the only way. he doesn't want to remember the broken chip-shop window, the cut hand, the same cut hand that smeared anna's face with a slap when she called him a stupid cunt. he doesn't want to remember his mum and dad when the police brought him home, the same mum and dad that are now sat downstairs waiting to talk to him, to cry and to shout, to tell him there is something wrong with him, to tell him that he's breaking their hearts and to ask in the name of good god all-bloody-chuffing-mighty: *why?*

Kate Rutter
Falling

My father's lost his marbles so it seems.
Today he tells me clearly he's been raped
which after days of incoherence means
at least a slight improvement. He gapes
and stares at me through green unseeing eyes.
Awful he says oh dear oh dear and
tries to drink a tissue, then he smiles.
I pour a drink and place it in his hand.
With effort he lifts up the trembling glass
then concentrates and looks into my face.
I like your little eyes he says, at last
remembering himself, his life, this place.
He lays his hands down neatly on the bed.
Icarus fell, he says, and bows his head.

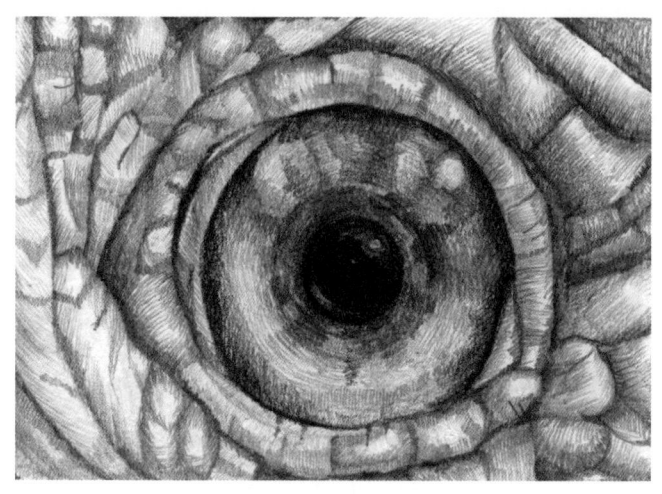

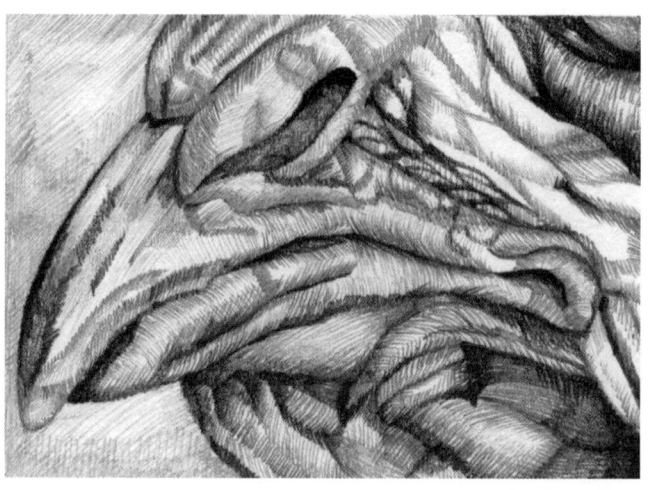

POETRY

Kate Rutter
Gretel's Nail

There was a trail of crumbs and we were together always together
which must have been annoying for him even though he loved me more
than you should love a sister on account of he knew someone had to.

As we travelled deeper in we did not know what we were looking for
that is until we saw it. That sugar house. That thing to suck on out there
in the middle of nowhere and the birds having eaten up any chance of home.

Her head tipped a bit to the side when she talked and her voice so gentle
but there was something about the way she licked him with her eyes and never
looked at me as she led us to sit by the stove to drink a little something for the cold.

I woke up to see him swinging there. Cursing me to wake up wake up get me down.
Strung up he was. The biggest canary I'd ever seen but my hands were bound
so tight this was no game we used to play. No game at all and where was she?

I could hear her singing out there. She was singing a rocking song. To no one.
Then in she came with firewood. He knew what it meant but I could never believe
in badness. That was my trouble he said. Always hoping for something.

I should have tried harder. Should have gnawed through the twine or freed a nail
from the truckle bed and worried at the rope that held his cage and felled it
like my father could fell a tree. Then he could have cracked her skull and run.

She feeds me now and when she's gone I sick it up for I must try to disappear.
There is only ever room for one of her. In my cage there is one loose nail
and I am working it like a tooth. Little by little by little.

SHORT STORY

Tricia Durdey
Queen of Puddings

We hang onto life by the skin of our teeth, by our passion, Catherine thought as she stood in the cool of her kitchen cracking eggs into the mixing basin. The door was open and outside on the veranda her husband, Max, lounged replete after his lunch, his fingers interlaced over the folds of his sun-tanned belly, his mouth slack. She might have told him he would wake with a sore head, sleeping in the midday sun, but he wouldn't listen. So be it. It was his concern. She would keep out of his way. Her kitchen was her refuge, the wooden table scrubbed smooth, the shining jars of pickles, conserves and spices, each labelled and dated and stacked in the larder. And in the dark recesses, hooked to the beams, the herbs she had gathered from the woods and stored upside down to dry. She learnt the name and healing property of each root and seed and berry.

It was almost too hot and still to breathe out there. The sound of laughter from the beach and the distant rumble of the sea seemed to hang in the air. If only the rain would come, maybe her mind would stop its torment and she could rest. She saw Max was awake now, ambling heavily over to the open door, his face flushed.

'Is there any coffee?'

'I'm busy. I'll make it soon.'

She would not look at him, though she felt him watching her. She concentrated on the stream of sugar as she poured it into the beaten egg. He came closer, slipping his hand between her legs, pleating her dress between his fingers. She froze. She gripped the white bowl.

'Don't do that.'

'Cold you are. Cold and anaemic as skimmed milk.'

'You're unkind.'

'Unkind!' he laughed. 'I'm very kind to put up with you at all. You've let yourself go, Catherine, you're a mess. You need help.'

If she kept very still he would go away.

Catherine had once believed in the possibility of love. Many times at dusk she stared at the darkening line of the ocean, her desolation so sharp it could stop her heart. Then Martha came.

Martha told everyone she was 'beginning a new life beside the ocean'. She lived her life as if she knew everyone admired her: Martha with her stories, her wild intrigues, her quick laughter. Catherine watched her, longed to know her better. Then they became friends. Over weeks Catherine told Martha everything, the story of her childhood, her dreams, her fears. And Martha listened.

Last Sunday, Catherine and Martha had climbed the cliff path back to Martha's cottage from the beach café. It was a starry evening and they flopped down drunk and breathless at the top.

'I adore life,' Martha said. 'The world is delicious, Catherine. Just look around you.' She drew deeply on her cigarette and flung her head back to look at the stars. The pulse throbbed in her slender neck. Catherine put out her hand. Martha was so beautiful and vital. The smell of her skin, the sound of her voice ...

'I love you,' she said. She had never said it before. 'You're the most beautiful person I've ever known.'

Martha took her hand, pressed it, and kissed her fingers with a theatrical gesture. She let her go.

'I love you too, honey! You're so mysterious. Deep dark

water, that's what you are.' She threw her cigarette butt into the grass.

The next day Catherine bought flowers for Martha, deep red roses, and stargazer lilies for their scent. She raced home neglecting the rest of her shopping. She would wash and change into the green dress that suited her so well, and go to Martha with the flowers. I'm going to leave Max, she would say. Then she and Martha would open a bottle of wine. They would embrace. She would tell Martha she was beginning a new life.

She arrived back early and thought the house was empty, but when she ran upstairs she heard Max's voice coming from his bedroom. There was someone with him. She stopped on the landing. She listened.

'You needn't think Catherine cares. She won't let me anywhere near her,' she heard him say. 'We haven't had sex for months.'

There was silence and then she heard Martha's laughter, intimate and unforgettable. She leant against the wall to stop herself falling.

'Why won't she let you anywhere near her? What's the matter with her? Is she frigid?' The breathless giggle again. 'Perhaps she's a lesbian. Have you thought of that, Max? You should leave her. You need better than that.'

That night Catherine slipped in and out of a fevered and terrible sleep, gripping the sheets in her teeth, grinding her fist into her belly. She dreamed of the White Bryony that grew rampant in the forest, the beautiful, delicate, poisonous flower. She was feeling her way through darkness until the plant bound her around with its tendrils, stopping all escape, its bright berries pressing their juices into her mouth. She was digging into the black earth, tearing at the root – the mandrake, until it screamed. She did not know if she was herself or Martha – the briny taste of Martha's warm mouth, the smell of her, rank and wild like the sea.

How hot and close it was even as the afternoon wore on, as if a storm were coming. Catherine opened the door of the larder and reached into the corner where the dried plants hung, feeling with her hands until her eyes became used to the gloom. Words pounded in her head, White Bryony, and its other names – Mandrake Root, Devil's Turnip, most bitter of purges.

The root lay twisted in her hand. She grated it into a dish and poured on water. She had invited Martha for dinner, and she was preparing the dessert. She stirred in the honey and the breadcrumbs. She reached for the cut glass bowls she and Max had been given for a wedding present. She was careful to put the mixture specifically into the bowl she would give to Martha, the one with the ruby red rim.

It began with darkness over the ocean, and then the rain swept across in sheets, water swirling onto the veranda from the guttering. Just before suppertime Martha ran down the lane from her cottage. She had forgotten her umbrella, she said, and her red silky dress clung wetly to her skin.

'Oh, I love the rain.' She held out her arms and turned her face to the sky. Max brought her a towel.

Indoors, Catherine lit the candles. The table was laid with the best linen and silver. The wine glasses were polished until they shone. They ate. Martha chattered; Max leaned back in his chair laughing with her. Catherine observed them. After dinner she cleared the plates and brought in the dessert in the cut glass bowls. She gave Martha the bowl with the ruby red rim.

'Queen of Puddings; it's bread crumbs mixed in an egg custard, and layers of berries and meringue.' Her voice sounded distant, disconnected.

'Queen of Puddings. I wonder why they called it that?'

Martha's voice rang out.

'I've no idea. It's Elizabethan, the recipe said.'

Martha began to eat and Catherine saw the slight frown as she tasted, an uncertainty clouding her eyes. She watched her swallow.

'Don't eat it if you don't like it.'

'No, it's fine.' Martha glanced at Max, saw him scraping his spoon around the empty bowl in satisfaction, and took another spoonful. Max pushed his chair away from the table.

'Anyone for a brandy?' he said. 'I'm having one.' He got up with an effort and shambled to the drinks cabinet.

Martha took another mouthful. Her bowl was nearly empty. She put down her spoon.

'You're very quiet tonight, Catherine. What is it? Tell me,' she said.

Catherine didn't speak. Martha touched her hand.

How strange. There was such affection, no suggestion of Martha's duplicity. For a moment, Catherine was beguiled. She longed so much to rest in the possibility of love. She held her gaze, those eyes she loved, then looked away. The rain beat against the window. Somewhere a door banged. She must not allow sentimentality. What was done was done.

'I've let myself go,' she said. She thrust Martha's hand away and stood up. Max turned, the brandy bottle in his hand. 'I'm as cold and anaemic as skimmed milk, as mysterious as dark water. I'm frigid. Perhaps I'm even a lesbian! It's what you both think, isn't it?'

As Catherine backed towards the door, she saw the look of bewilderment in Martha's face change to one of dismay.

'Whatever I am, you'll find that where cooking's concerned I know exactly what I'm doing.'

She left the room and ran out across the garden to the car. She started the engine.

Martha would start to feel the terrible griping pain soon.

It would make her writhe in agony and there would be no relief. She would long to be dead. As Catherine backed the car out of the drive, she saw Max running towards her through the rain. He was shouting. He looked quite mad.

She'd cut off the phone. There'd be nobody to help. Martha would be alone with him. She began to laugh.

She drove away into the dark. She drove through the night.

POETRY

Jamie Coward
The Coxcomb

That a gentleman would call at
the house of another gentleman
is well recorded. That

he would hand off his hat,
gloves and cane to the man
in the hall is accepted as fact.

What happened to the hat
and to some extent the cane
can be comfortably guessed at:

one imagines a hook on a wall,
a stand or closet of some kind
in a shadowy part of the hall,

but what came of the gloves, ritually
folded and paired, lies beyond
the reach of social history.

Were they placed, by the factotum,
in the carefully labelled drawer
of an understairs compactium

reserved for that purpose,
or did the faithful valet,
inscrutably deep in his cups,

separate the gloves, mating them
with others in his stud,
for sheer amusement.

Or did he take them to the parlour,
knowing the master would have approved,
there to strut before the mirror,

one glove balanced atop
his brilliantined head,
mimicking a cock.

NON FICTION

Diana Gabaldon
Remember the Alamo

From October of 1835 to April of 1836, the settlers of Texas y Coahuila fought a military campaign for independence from Mexico. The only part of this campaign that anyone remembers is the siege and final battle at the Alamo, a decommissioned mission church in which a hundred or so Texian defenders held out for 12 days against five thousand soldiers of General Santa Anna's Mexican Army. Not surprisingly, they lost. Everything.

In May of 1990, I was at a writer's conference in San Antonio, staying at the Menger Hotel, a rather charming old place built in the late 1800s. It's also located across the street from the Alamo, which now stands in a little botanical park, full of trees and shrubs, each with a little metal label bearing its name.

A friend had driven up from Houston to see me, and he suggested that we go walk through the Alamo, he being a botanist and, therefore, interested in the plants outside. He also thought I might find the building interesting. He said he'd been there several times as a child, and had found it 'evocative.' So we strolled through the garden, looking at ornamental cabbages, and then went inside.

The present memorial is the single main church building, which is essentially no more than a gutted masonry shell. There's nothing at all in the church proper – a stone floor and stone walls, bearing the marks of hundreds of thousands of bullets; the stone looks chewed. There are a couple of smaller semi-open rooms at the front of the church, where the baptismal font and a small chapel used to be; these are separated from the main room by stone pillars and partial walls.

Around the edges of the main room are a few museum display cases, holding such artifacts of the defenders as the Daughters of Texas have managed to scrape together – rather a pitiful collection, including spoons, buttons, and (scraping the bottom of the barrel, if you ask me) a diploma certifying that one of the defenders had graduated from law school (this, like a number of other artifacts there, wasn't present in the Alamo during the battle, but was obtained later from the family of the man to whom it belonged).

The walls are lined with execrable oil paintings, showing various of the defenders in assorted 'heroic' poses. I suspect them all of having been executed by the Daughters of Texas in a special arts-and-crafts class held for the purpose, though I admit that I might be maligning the D of T by this supposition. At any rate, as museums go, this one doesn't.

It is quiet – owing to the presence of the woman waving the 'Silence, Please! THIS IS A SHRINE!' sign in the middle of the room – but is not otherwise either spooky or reverent in atmosphere. It's just a big, empty room. My friend and I cruised slowly around the room, making *sotto voce* remarks about the paintings and looking at the artifacts.

And then I walked into a ghost. He was near the front of the main room, about ten feet in from the wall, near the smaller room on the left (as you enter the church). I was surprised by this encounter, since a) I'd never met a ghost before; b) I hadn't expected to meet a ghost right then, and c) if I had, he wasn't what I would have expected.

I saw nothing, experienced no chill or feeling of oppression or malaise. The air felt slightly warmer where I stood, but not so much as to be really noticeable. The only really distinct feeling was one of ... communication. Very distinct communication. I *knew* he was there – and he certainly knew *I* was. It was the feeling you get when you meet the eyes of a stranger and know at once this is someone you'd like.

I wasn't frightened in the least; just intensely surprised. I had a strong urge to continue standing there, 'talking' (as it were; there were no words exchanged then) to this – man. Because it *was* a man; I could 'feel' him distinctly, and had a strong sense of his personality. I rather naturally assumed that I was imagining this, and turned to find my friend, to re-establish a sense of reality. He was about six feet away, and I started to walk toward him. Within a couple of feet, I lost contact with the ghost; couldn't feel him anymore. It was like leaving someone at a bus stop; a sense of broken communication.

Without speaking to my friend, I turned and went back to the spot where I had encountered the ghost. There he was. Again, he was quite conscious of me, too, though he didn't say anything in words. It was a feeling of 'Oh, there you are!' on both parts.

I tried the experiment two or three more times – stepping away and coming back – with similar results each time. If I moved away, I couldn't feel him; if I moved back, I could. By this time, my friend was becoming understandably curious. He came over and whispered, 'Is this what a writer does?' meaning to be funny. Since he evidently didn't sense the ghost – he was standing approximately where I had been – I didn't say anything about it, but merely smiled and went on outside with him, where we continued our botanical investigations.

The whole occurrence struck me as so very odd – while at the same time feeling utterly 'normal' – that I went back to the Alamo – alone, this time – on each of the next two days. Same thing; he was there, in the same spot, and he knew me. Each time, I would just stand there, engaged in what I can only call mental communication. As soon as I left the spot – it was an area maybe two to three feet square – I couldn't sense him anymore.

I did wonder who he was, of course. There are brass plates at intervals around the walls of the church, listing the vital statistics of all the Alamo defenders, and I'd strolled along looking at these, trying to see if any of them rang a psychic bell, so to speak. None did.

Now, I did mention the occurrence to a few of the writers at the conference, all of whom were very interested. I don't think any of them went to the Alamo themselves – if they did, they didn't tell me – but more than one of them suggested that perhaps the ghost wanted me to tell his story, I being a writer and all. I said dubiously that I didn't *think* that's what he wanted, but the next – and last – time I went to the Alamo, I did ask him, in so many words.

I stood there and thought – consciously, in words – 'What do you want? I can't really do anything for you. All I can give you is the knowledge that I know you're there; I care that you lived and I care that you died here.'

And he *said* – not out loud, but I heard the words distinctly inside my head; it was the only time he spoke – he said 'That's enough.'

At once, I had a feeling of completion. It *was* enough; that's all he wanted. I turned and went away. This time, I took a slightly different path out of the church, because there was a group of tourists in my way. Instead of leaving in a straight line to the door, I passed around the pillar dividing the main church from one of the smaller rooms. There was a small brass plate in the angle of the wall there, not visible from the main room.

The plate said that the smaller room had been used as a powder magazine during the defence of the fort. During the last hours of the siege, when it became apparent that the fort would fall, one of the defenders had made an effort to blow up the magazine, in order to destroy the fort and take as many of the attackers as possible with it. However, the man had been shot and killed just outside the smaller room, before he could succeed in his mission – more or less on the spot where I met the ghost.

So I don't know for sure; he didn't tell me his name, and I got no clear idea of his appearance – just a general impression that he was fairly tall; he spoke 'down' to me, somehow. But for what it's worth, the man who was killed trying to blow up the powder magazine was named Robert Evans; he was described as being 'black-haired, blue-eyed, nearly six feet tall, and always merry.' That last bit sounds like the man I met, all right, but there's no telling.

CHILDREN'S FICTION EXTRACT

Noel Williams
from How to Kill Francesca. Twice.

Chapter One

'I don't care what kinds of demon are after you, you can't come in here.'

Topaz, tall, elegant and snarling, spread her wings to block the entrance to her slowly spinning cave.

'I'm really, really important,' wheedled Panjak, fluttering his wings faster than a hummingbird to keep level with the asteroid.

Panjak bumped against her, trying to thrust past into the cavern. But Topaz was tall and strong for a 13-year-old demon. Her wings, though still downy, were tough. Panjak bounced off.

'And I don't care what sort of demon you are, either,' her amber eyes blazed. 'Actually, what sort of demon are you?'

Panjak looked down at himself. He knew he resembled a slightly inflated beetroot. If beetroots had wings and a tail.

'That's not important – just let me in. They're searching Outermost Helle today. I know it.'

'Go away,' Topaz said. 'I'm very busy.'

'Of course you are – me too.' Panjak looked up at the gawky teen demon in his way. 'You're very tall.'

'You're very short. Get away from my cave before I make you even shorter.' But Panjak noticed she preened the golden fur across her forehead, distracted by his remark.

'Oh look,' he exclaimed, 'an exploding comet!'

He gestured with a fiery spark from his tail. For a

moment, Topaz glanced across the blackness of space, filled with the tumbling rocks that rumbled together in Helle's Furthest Circle.

'Where?' she said. 'I don't see ...'

It was all he needed. Panjak rolled his wings around him in a spiky ball and cannoned between Topaz's legs into the cave. The whole rock shuddered as he tumbled across a white marble floor, scattering a heap of diamonds.

'Hey!' She swung her claws round menacingly, but he was too quick.

'Got to hide. Got to hide.'

Panjak scurried around the crimson cavern, knocking over piles of parchment, tripping over a pure white stalagmite.

'Cool cave,' he remarked, as he scuttled around, leaping over fissures and upturning carved slabs as he looked for a serious place to hide. 'Hey! What's that?'

Topaz swooped low across the cave to snatch at him. But he ducked under her arms, scampering up a mound of veined rock to her observatory, which quivered at the top. On a cradle of gold and silver, a hollow globe of wires and discs spun, glittering with diamonds. In the middle of the whole apparatus sat one fat and glorious jewel, cracked but starlight beautiful. The device was so big that Panjak could probably have squeezed inside it. But it was useless as a hiding place.

'What is that?' he cried. 'I've never seen one of these before.'

'It's an Occluscope. It's the only one. I made it. Get down! Don't touch it!'

Panjak scrambled onto the saddle of rock that made a seat, and squinted into the great diamond. Through a split in the wall he gazed out into space, out to the slowly spinning stars. And beyond the stars, a million miles away but magnified unnaturally by the jewel, a brilliant blue planet.

'Wow!' he said.

Topaz looped the loop, and flew towards him, rippling silken wings.

'Don't touch,' she screamed. 'I've just found the azimuth …'

Rolling over with one elegant flap of her wings, she swooped down upon him. It would have been perfect if Panjak hadn't leapt out of the way, plunging into the delicate mechanism as she came. As she rose again to the high roof at the centre of the cavern, she hooked her tail into his.

'Got you!' she screamed.

Panjak squeaked, as she hauled him out of the golden discs, which spun and screeched as he grabbed hold of them.

'Let go!' she cried out. 'You'll spoil everything.'

'You let go,' he cried back, 'or I will.'

And then, flickering but bright, a spar of light shot through the diamond lens, blazing the image of the blue sphere upon the ceiling. It grew and grew. First, a planet, dizzy with cloud. Then, a porridge of seas and islands.

Topaz pulled. Panjak pulled. The gold discs squealed.

Then: a fist of mountains, holding tight to a city. Then: a crossword of streets and blacked-in buildings.

She tried a different tack, bending down to haul on his tail with her hands as well as her own tail. But she lost height this way. He slipped back into the Occluscope.

Then: a city square, in the dark of deep night, crisscrossed by the headlights of manoeuvering buses. Then: a girl at a table in a café, forlorn, chewing her hair, watching her companion as he hesitantly explained something, nervously, a black box in his hand.

Then, the great diamond came away in Panjak's hands. Suddenly released, the two young demons shot up towards the ceiling, racing towards the image of the girl at the café table. The whole picture vanished.

'Is that Earth?' Panjak asked, as he tumbled to the ground, hugging the diamond to his chest and completely forgetting to fly.

'I told you not to touch it. Look what you've done!'

Topaz recovered quickly. She swooped down below him, caught him as he neared the ground, ripped the diamond from his grasp and dropped him to the floor.

'Oof!' he said, clambering to his feet. 'No need to be so rough. I've never seen Earth before.'

He was sparkling with diamond dust like a disco glitterball. He brushed at his hide.

'I've heard lots about it,' he continued. 'I've seen carvings, of course. Tidal waves. Dandelions. Neopolitan ice cream. Wow, this stuff is cool …'

He began to prance around the cave, looking over his shoulder at the shine of his tail.

'You've never seen Earth?'

'Let me look properly.'

'No way, blubber-boy. You've nearly destroyed my most important experiment. It'll take ages to get it right again. I might not have time now. If you've stopped me killing Francesca …'

'Just let me have a proper look.'

Panjak grabbed at the diamond. Topaz held him at bay. He fluttered his stubby wings madly, bumbling around her. With her deft movements she held him off, shaking her head.

'Get someone else to show you,' she said. 'I've no time for Africa. I've no time for frozen waterfalls or sticky toffee pudding. I've no time for hopscotch. I've got to set that azimuth again, before it's too late.'

'Why are you wasting time talking about it if you don't have time? And what is sticky toffee pudding, anyway? Is it very sticky?'

'Hey! In the middle of something here, bilge-breath. Do you not understand? You're in the way. Get out. Go away.

There. Doorway. Space. Flee.'

'I want to see Earth.'

'You won't see your own tail again if you carry on like this, porkling. I could bounce you out of here like a rubber moon.'

'Just try it. I'm pretty magic, you know.' The tip of Panjak's tail flickered with fire. 'What was that?'

Outside the cave came a rustling and a flapping, as if a clutch of great bats had settled on the slowly turning rock. Then a scraping sound, the sound of the sharpening of claws.

'Quick! Hide me!'

Panjak rushed across the cave, overturning a scroll-case, knocking down a model of Inner Helle, looking for a cleft wide enough to hide him.

'He's in here!' cried Topaz.

RADIO PLAY EXTRACT

Tanya Chan-Sam
from Motjie's Samoosas

Characters

Motjie:	45, widow, Muslim, housewife, educated.
Dinah:	indeterminate age, homeless, bergie (mountain dweller/vagrant).
Bea:	38, Motjie's neighbour, rival.
Sedick:	45, small time drug dealer, Motjie and Bea's lover.
Mr D:	60, drugs boss, disillusioned, loves Pavarotti.
Skollie:	38, street corner drug dealer.
Henchman:	32, slow-witted.
Waiter:	25, impatient.

Notes: Music
Dinah's voiceover – indigenous Southern African one-stringed harp with plaintive sound.
Mr D house and car scenes – Pavarotti arias.
Love scene between Motjie and Sedick – R&B soul sound.
Car scenes with Motjie, Bea and Dinah – muted commercial radio station.

Scene 1: INTRODUCTION. CAPE TOWN STREET.
Night urban sound. Background wind, cars driving on wet roads. (Fade in music, focus on music then bring down to run under narration)

DINAH v/o: *(drunk)* Ja djy, yes you, kom hierso. Sit here by Dinah. Ag don' pull your face like that. Met'lated spirits keep me young. And is raining again. My cardboard's all wet. I won't sleep tonight. But at least I got lekker samoosas. You want one? Is from Motjie's Cafe, you know there by the Waterfront. That nice one with the blue tables outside. Ja, she mus gimme! She keep my money mos. She invest it for me, she say. I say, ja, ja, jus inves' properly. You want to know how I come to be a investor, huh? It all start with Sedick. Tch, that Sedick. Is two, three years ago now. I see him that afternoon in Sea Point. I watch him go into Mr D's house. **(fade out music)**

Scene 2: MR D'S Study. (Fade in Pavarotti under rhythmic slap of wads of notes)

MR D: 60, 70, 80, 90, five hundred thousand rand.
SEDICK: It's all there, Mr D.
MR D: I'm taking a big risk on you, Sedick.
SEDICK: You gonna see, Boss, I'm ready for it.
MR D: Let's run through it one last time.
SEDICK: Ok, I tell the Nigerian I'm setting up on my own and I want him to be my supplier. I already control the corners in Woodstock.
MR D: Let *him* ask the questions. Don't offer too much information. He must *not* know you work for me.
SEDICK: Ok, Mr D.
MR D: *(pause)* We can both make a lot of money here.
SEDICK: With this deal I could be off the street corners by tomorrow.
MR D: Ja well, do the deal first. I want you back by seven o' clock.
SEDICK: No problem.

Scene 3: **OUTSIDE MR D'S HOUSE.**
(Late afternoon. Urban traffic. Sea gulls. Car alarm disengaged)

DINAH: **(on)** *(drunk)* Here's my Mr Sedick. I did watch your car. Lemme carry your bag.

SEDICK: **(on)** Leave it!

DINAH: I jus' put it in the boot for you, Mr Sedick.

SEDICK: **(click of boot opening)** I'll do it myself.

DINAH: What's wrong, huh?

SEDICK: Go away! You stink!

DINAH: Oh, cos I stink I can't help. Other times you don't mind.

SEDICK: Get outta my sight.

DINAH: I jus' close the boot for a small one rand.

SEDICK: No!

DINAH: Voetsek! I don' even want to carry your bag.

SEDICK: Good!

DINAH What you got in there anyway?

SEDICK: None of your bladdy business.

DINAH: I did look nicely after your car, Mr Sedick.

SEDICK: Don't lie! You sat on the pavement and drank meths. Sies!

DINAH: Haai, I always watch your car and I watch for you *(lowers voice)* and for Motjie. I always watch.

SEDICK: **(clicks teeth)** What you want?

DINAH: A little something, please.

SEDICK: **(coins chink)** Here.

DINAH: A whole 50 cents, Mr Sedick!

SEDICK: Must be your lucky day. **(door opens, closes, ignition, car drives off)**

DINAH: Cheapskate! 50 cents is jus' shrapnel. It won' even buy a loose cigarette. **(sucks teeth)** Jerre, I mus now walk in the rain to Motjie to get food. That's far, man. All the way from Sea Point to At'lone.

Scene 4: **MOTJIE'S KITCHEN. (Hissing sound of frying. Utensils clanking. Heavy dance beat music in background)**

MOTJIE: **(on)** I can't hear myself think with that racket next door. They carry on like it's the weekend. **(knock)** At last a customer. **(going with Motjie)** I'm coming. **(door opens)**

MOTJIE: Oh, it's you, Dinah.
DINAH: *(drunk)* **(a little off)** Hallo, Motjie.
MOTJIE: What do you want?
DINAH: Can I come in? *(pause)* It's raining hard and I did walk all –
MOTJIE: You can't stay long. I'm busy. **(door closes, utensils clink)**
DINAH: *(pause)* **(on)** Sjoe, that's better, it's warm in here. Mmmm. The samoosas smell lekker, Motjie.
MOTJIE: I can't give you today, Dinah.
DINAH: I'm hungry, Motjie. I walk all the way from Sea Point.
MOTJIE: And obviously got lekker drunk along the way.
DINAH: Not a drop pass my lips.
MOTJIE: Dinah, you absolutely reek.
DINAH: I swear onna bible.
MOTJIE: Dinah! God will punish you.
DINAH: I'm hungry, Motjie. *(pause)* And that Sedick didn't help me. Motjie mus talk with him. *(pause)* **(louder)** You hear what I say?
MOTJIE: Don't shout. There's nothing wrong with my ears.
DINAH: Ag only two small samoosas, asseblief.
MOTJIE: Dinah, these are my last samoosas. I have to sell them.
DINAH: Jinne, Motjie, I las' ate –
MOTJIE: Last Christmas, I know. Dinah, you don't understand.

DINAH:	What don' I understand, Motjie?
MOTJIE:	You don't know what it's like to worry about money, rent, food.
DINAH:	I aw'so worry. Today I only got 50 cents. I need jus' so a little bit more then I can stop worrying.
MOTJIE:	You'll buy more methylated spirits.
DINAH:	I don't drink that stuff, Motjie!
MOTJIE:	Dinah, you'd burst into flames if you came near a match.
DINAH:	Is cold tonight, Motjie. A rand, jus to buy bread, please?
MOTJIE:	I haven't got truly. I'm waiting for someone to bring me money.
DINAH:	Ok, then I wait.
MOTJIE:	What are you waiting for?
DINAH:	For Motjie's connection to come with the money mos.
MOTJIE:	You've got a cheek!
DINAH:	Herre, but someone is crabby today. I rather go nex' door to Bea. At leas' there's a lekker party there.
MOTJIE:	Oh, you want to spite me. Leave and close my door.
DINAH:	Look how ugly it get now. *(pause)* Motjie can maar skel, but I will never leave my Motjie.
MOTJIE:	Go to the party, Dinah. I'm busy. **(clanging utensils, crockery)**
DINAH:	*(a beat)* Bea will give on credit if someone can sponsor me.
MOTJIE:	Isn't it enough she steals from me? Now she'll take you too.
DINAH:	She can't steal me, Motjie.
MOTJIE:	Yes, she steals my customers.
DINAH:	Haai, a person can't steal customers.

MOTJIE:	She stole my customers with her big boobs and bums hanging out all over the street.
DINAH:	Oooh, hear now the skinder, tell me more, what did she do?
MOTJIE:	Every dog's arse that stretches, she's up it, but she's mos your friend!
DINAH:	*(cackles)* Haai, Motjie, don' be jillus.
MOTJIE:	I'm not jealous! She knows I struggle but suddenly she must also sell samoosas. Why?
DINAH:	She jus' like you. She also struggle.
MOTJIE:	Struggle? Her? She sells dagga, and keeps a loose house. Siss she's a disgrace. **(screams. loud thuds background)**
DINAH:	**(close, whisper)** What's happening?
MOTJIE:	**(lowered tone)** Bea and Paulie next door, they're fighting again.
DINAH:	She got a hard life, that Bea.
MOTJIE:	She deserves it.
DINAH:	How you mean?
MOTJIE:	She's got loose elastic on her panties.
DINAH:	Oooh, listen to you. Your mouth full of chillies again **(louder screams from next door)** Bea is getting hit.
MOTJIE	**(off) (tap running)** Good, *(laughs)* about time Paulie puts his foot down.
DINAH:	Hey, Motjie, you mus'n' say that, you the kinda woman who never get hit.
MOTJIE:	My husband, Allah rest his soul, never lifted his hand and that's because he never had anything to worry about.
DINAH:	Faried was a good man. So sad he die so young, and poor little Rashaad. Oh, my heart is still so sore.
MOTJIE:	Dinah, please, I don't want to talk about Rashaad. If Faried was alive I wouldn't have to

	put up with them next door. I wouldn't even be living here.
DINAH:	*(sighs)* I know, Motjie.
MOTJIE:	That Bea is like a cat on nylon stockings, up and down the street, throwing her hips around, her eyes all over the men.
DINAH:	But she's young and jus full of juice.
MOTJIE:	Hopefully she will have no juice and be so sore tomorrow she won't sell her samoosas. Then at least I can get some of my customers back.
DINAH:	Yunnow, I do love you, Motjie, but sometimes your tongue can cut a person open. Don't be so nasty.
MOTJIE:	Go to your friend if you're so concerned about her. **(utensils clinking)**
BEA:	**(banging on door)** Open up! Maak oop asseblief! **(door bursts open)**
DINAH:	Herre Gott! Bea!
BEA:	He gonna kill me!
MOTJIE:	Oh my god! Look!
BEA:	Close the door!
DINAH:	Hoelie ha! Your face!
BEA:	Close it! **(door bangs shut)**
MOTJIE	She's got a gun!
DINAH:	Your face! The blood!
BEA:	I mus hide! Oh herre, I mus hide.
DINAH:	Bea! Bea!
BEA:	He's coming!
DINAH:	Is me, Dinah.
BEA:	He's right behind me!
MOTJIE:	Who's coming?!
BEA:	Paulie!
DINAH:	Point the gun the other way, Bea.
MOTJIE:	Lock the door, Dinah. **(key turns in lock)**

BEA:	Help me, please.
DINAH:	Why you got a gun? Did you do something?
BEA:	No! It's Paulie's gun.
DINAH:	Then why you got it?
BEA:	He said he gonna shoot me and then he's gonna —
MOTJIE:	Where's Paulie now?
BEA:	Gone to look for someone.
MOTJIE:	Thank god he's gone. Come sit. **(chair scrapes on floor)**
BEA:	Thanks, Motjie. **(sighs, whimpers)** He said he's gonna kill him.
DINAH:	What?
MOTJIE:	I don't want to hear about killing in my house.
DINAH:	Who's he gonna kill?
MOTJIE:	Dinah, Bea's bleeding.
DINAH:	Haai shame, Bea. Your face.
MOTJIE	Dinah, we must clean all this blood off her.
DINAH:	Your eye is swollen.
MOTJIE:	Move her hand off the table, Dinah. That's a nasty cut on her finger.
BEA:	*(cries)* I can see nothing outta my lef' eye.
MOTJIE:	I can't bear to look.
DINAH:	You mus' put raw meat on it. Motjie, get a steak from your freezer.
MOTJIE:	Don't be forward, Dinah! **(clicks teeth)**
BEA:	*(tearful)* We were having such a lekker party.
MOTJIE:	Mmm, we heard, hey, Dinah?
BEA:	Paulie jus' skielik got stupid and jillus.
MOTJIE:	Ja well, men and liquor, hey. **(going)** I'll get Dettol from the bathroom. Dinah, put water in a bowl.
DINAH:	**(close. lowered voice)** Why did he hit you, Bea?
	(tap running)

BEA:	**(close)** *(whispers)* He found out.
DINAH:	*(whispers)* What?
BEA:	Don' tell Motjie ne.
DINAH:	Uh huh, I won'.
BEA:	She like to judge a person. She very.
DINAH	What did he find out!
BEA:	*(pause)* I got a boyfriend.
DINAH:	Jou diep skelm. How did he find out?
BEA:	He lissun when I was talking on the phone.
DINAH:	And?
MOTJIE:	**(off)** Do you need plasters, Bea?
BEA:	I tell you later.
MOTJIE:	**(approaching)** Here's the Dettol. Dinah, wash Bea's face.
DINAH:	Motjie, no man, I can't.
MOTJIE:	Dinah, you know I can't bear to touch blood.
DINAH:	My stomach feel full of hairy worms when I see blood and goeters, Motjie.
MOTJIE:	You of all people should know I can't stand blood!
DINAH:	I know, Motjie. But the blood, man. I can't evens look.
MOTJIE:	Dinah, it happened right here in my kitchen. Rashaad lay here there. You were here that day when my boy. And the blood. My boy ...
DINAH:	Ooh, Motjie, you make me heartsore now. *(pause)* Bea, haven't you got a beer to calm my nerves?
MOTJIE:	Dinah! How can you think of liquor now?
DINAH:	Motjie, I need a little something.
MOTJIE:	Just help the woman! Wipe the blood off her.
DINAH:	For my nerves, please, Motjie. You can pay Bea later.
MOTJIE:	I won't give money for liquor!
BEA:	Herre, Dinah, stop begging her. I'll give you the

	beer later.
DINAH:	Thank you very much, Bea! Lift your face, bokkie.
BEA:	Ooh! Eina!
DINAH:	Keep still, Bea.
BEA:	Ouch! You making me sore!
MOTJIE:	*(lowered tone)* Shush, I can hear something.
DINAH:	What?
MOTJIE:	*(whisper)* Footsteps. Outside.
BEA:	*(whisper)* Is Paulie!
MOTJIE:	Turn off the lights. He'll think I'm not here.
BEA:	He gonna fin' me here. He gonna kill me.
MOTJIE:	Dinah! Turn off the lights. **(click)** **(knock – three knocks, interval, three knocks)**
BEA:	He know I'm here!
DINAH:	Motjie?
MOTJIE:	Shush!
	(Knock repeated, louder)
BEA:	Motjie, I'm scared. What we gonna do?
MOTJIE:	Hide in the lounge. I'll talk to him
BEA:	What you gonna say?
MOTJIE:	I'll tell him –
BEA:	Say I'm not here.
DINAH:	Motjie?
BEA:	Say to Paulie you never even saw me the whole day.
DINAH:	Motjie?
MOTJIE:	Wait, Dinah!
BEA:	**(going)** Say you didn' see me the whole week.
DINAH:	Motjie?
MOTJIE:	What is it, Dinah!
DINAH:	I mus go now.
MOTJIE:	What?

DINAH:	When Paulie come in, I jus' slip out when you open the door.
MOTJIE	Are you mad?
DINAH:	And then Motjie can mos talk to him.
MOTJIE:	Get in that lounge!
DINAH:	**(going) (clicks teeth)** Haai man, Motjie man. *(pause)* **(Knock)**
MOTJIE:	**(close)** Who is it?
SEDICK:	It's me. Open up. **(key unlocks. door opens)**
MOTJIE:	*(whisper)* Sedick!
SEDICK:	Expecting someone else?
MOTJIE	You can't come in.
SEDICK:	Why not?
MOTJIE:	*(whisper)* I … it's just, I'm not ready for you.
SEDICK:	*(lowers voice)* **(close)** But the lights are out, looks like you in the mood already.
MOTJIE:	*(whisper)* Sssh, keep your voice down.
SEDICK:	**(seductive)** Want me to whisper? Come here.
MOTJIE:	Sedick, no!
SEDICK:	**(speaking into her neck, muffled)** You smell lekker.
MOTJIE:	Not now!
SEDICK:	Now's exac'ly when I want you, bokkie. **(kisses)**
MOTJIE:	Just let me say something.
SEDICK:	What?
MOTJIE:	Leave my buttons alone!
SEDICK:	Relax. I know how to do it.
MOTJIE:	There's something I have to tell **(voice peters out)** you.
SEDICK:	I love your mouth. **(kissing)**
MOTJIE:	Oh god.
SEDICK:	And your –
MOTJIE:	Sedick! Wait.
SEDICK:	**(going)** Come here

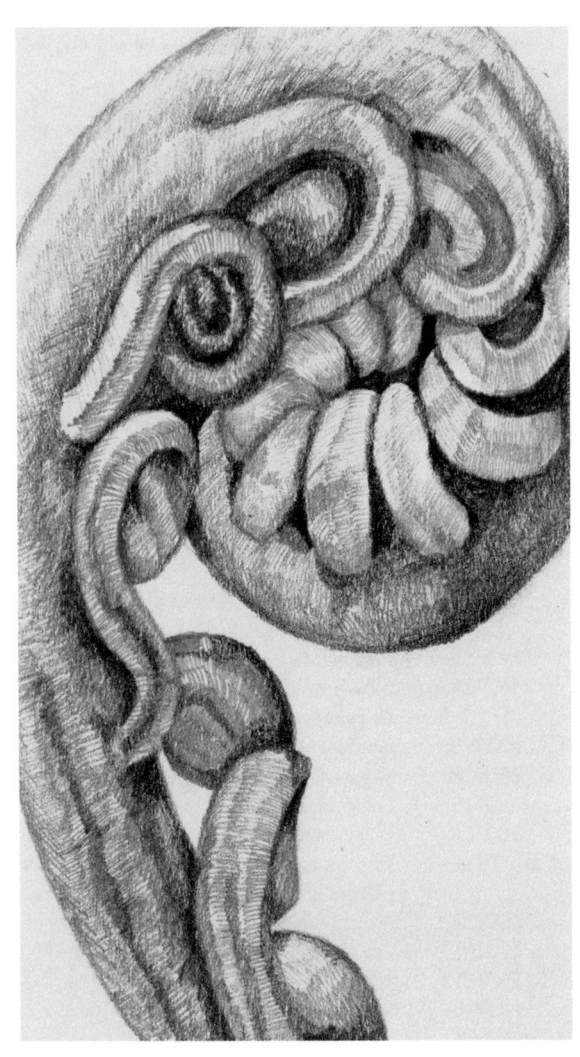

POETRY

Suzannah Evans
Rut

The morning is a wet wax jacket,
the bracken flat from days of fights.

Two bucks belch between the pines,
antlers held up, stiff palmed hands.

Knees bend as they lock heads, dance,
taunt in grunts. Shoulders twitch

in stalemate. Only the mist shifts
until the smallest shrugs, slips the knot,

lets the other stagger against an absent weight.

Elisabeth Von Aster
from Can Lobsters Swim?

The Scientist

There weren't any crumbs on the white stone table. Daniel was eating breakfast. He looked at the date on the newspaper, opened his notebook and wrote:

Friday, 19/07/96: Investigation misson was a disaster. Need to be more careful! Kocas have a girl. She is crazy. She must go to the village school, with Silvano and Alex. The living room window is a good spot for spying. The flat is well ugly. Photos everywhere. Old furnitshur and not tidy. Small.

His mom was doing the dishes. He had not told her about the girl. She did not know about his experiments and investigations, either. He had once showed her a picture in a magazine of a man in a scientist's lab coat and said that his father was just as clever as this guy. 'Don't be silly,' she had said.

He was prepared to be told off at the shop. In bed last night he had thought of possible excuses for getting caught in Koca's flat. He got lost. He heard a suspicious noise upstairs and had a look. He had the runs and needed to toilet but did not want to mention it out of embarrassment, and searched for another toilet in what he thought was their flat upstairs. Diabetes might be better. Yes, he had diabetes and was embarrassed and had to find a safe place to give himself an emergency injection. He once saw his teacher, Mrs. Seibli, give Mark an injection in the boy's toilet.

Easy. The problem was what he had told the girl: 'lunch is

ready'. That would not fit with his excuse.

He found it difficult to chew and swallow his bread and honey; he knew the feeling of having told a lie. It's not the act of lying he was bothered about, but the humiliation that comes with being found out. Because being caught lying meant that you can't do anything but admit that what you were doing was wrong. And he agonised when that familiar feeling crept up his throat. It came every time he realised that the consequences of having told a particular lie are impossible to overcome with another lie.

Maggie draped Daniel's custom-made apron around his neck and fastened the strings around his waist by tying them into a knot at his back. He stood as still as he could, expecting her to tie them up painfully tight. But she did not. As she finished, she turned him around and mumbled 'you did a fine job yesterday.'

Still having her hands on his shoulders, she turned him around again, and gave him a little shove into the direction of the storeroom, where Koca was waiting for him.

He had a price-gun in his hand. He pointed it towards him. Daniel could not figure out the expression on Koca's face.

'Pow!'

Koca pressed the lever and the price-gun made a tiny 'click'. He laughed.

'I will show you how to price things today.'

His task was to stick price tags onto goods and fill up the shelves with them where needed. Koca had prepared a handwritten list with the price of each of the objects in the boxes in front of him. He learned how to turn the tiny gearwheels on the gun so that they printed the right digits. It was a fiddly task and kept him focused until Maggie told him to have a break. It was ten o'clock by then. There had only been one customer in; the lady from the photography shop bought some milk and biscuits. She stayed for a full 20 minutes, though, as Koca listened to her account of her dog's tragic death.

Daniel sat on the bench in the corridor eating a chocolate croissant and sipping an orange juice. He had been allowed to pick anything he wanted out of the shop for a snack. By then he was sure that the girl had not told her parents about their encounter. He glanced at the door leading to the flat upstairs. It was shut this time.

'You can go and see Ida after you've done your work.'

Daniel looked at Koca with a start.

'She'll be happy to see you.'

Oh no. He *did* know.

He felt the conversation wasn't over yet, but he didn't know what to say.

'There is nothing to be ashamed of for being curious, boy. You didn't need to have to tell a lie,' Koca said.

Daniel could not help but be curious. After he finished his chores, he took out his notebook, ready for a second go at investigating.

'I'm going upstairs now,' he called, and received an approving nod from Koca.

This time he found the apartment to be lighter. The opening to the attic was shut. The light came from one of the bedroom windows. It was wide open and made its drawn-back curtains flutter. He went to inspect. It seemed to be the girl's bedroom. Pink stuff. And a doll's pram in the corner. There was probably a doll in there. He felt tempted to follow the curious urge to see what the doll looked like, when he heard a sneeze. It came from outside. The window faced out to the backyard. As he poked his head out, he saw Ida sitting on a porch roof. It had no banister. It was pretty high. Ida sat on a towel, wearing a green dress. She looked more normal this time.

'Hello,' she said, 'I am drawing a picture.'

'How did you get down there?'

'Oh, I am actually not allowed to be here. Mama says it's too dangerous. But Papa comes here sometimes. To smoke the smelly ones.' He noticed a semi-hidden ashtray filled with cigar butts next to the chimney.

'You have to use that.' She pointed at a rope tied to the window slat. It was hanging down the tiles, leading to the tin roof. She placed her hand on her forehead to shield her eyes from the fierce sunlight. 'It needs a lot of practice.'

Daniel was up for the challenge. He climbed onto the windowsill and stood up straight holding onto the window frame. He pretended he did this kind of roof climbing every day. He bent his knees and grabbed the rope. He held on to it as strongly as he could so that his fingers turned white and hurt a little. His first backward step onto the roof tiles was immensely scary, but two steps later he reached the safety of the two-square-metre tin roof. He copied Ida and sat down onto the first line of tiles, resting his feet on the tin roof. The brick tiles, heated up by the sun, were burning under his bottom. That's why she was sitting on a towel.

'I knew you could do that. Being good at sneaking means being good at climbing.'

And then she focused back on her drawing. She sketched the tree in the yard, the branches of which were only a few inches from the tin roof. He could have touched them if he went closer to the edge, but he did not dare to move.

If that is what you do up here, be quiet and do a project, I will do so too, he thought. He took out his notebook and wrote in the tiniest writing possible,

2nd investigation. Koca's flat. Secret inspekshon of what to collect. Must be very secret, girl can't know. Must be small objects.

Perhaps the size of that pink eraser he saw on Ida's desk. So anything smaller than his little finger. He looked at his little finger. It had a large mole right in the middle of it. He wondered why fingers were different sizes.

'What are you writing?'

'None of your business.'

'I've noticed you write in that book before. You always wrote in it before you took something from the shelves.'

'How do you know?'

'Because I've got a cave in the shop.'

'A cave?'

'Yeah, I'll show you.'

She climbed back inside, and Daniel followed, glad to be off the roof. She told him to take off his shoes. As he did so, Ida, who had been barefoot on the tin roof, put on some socks.

'Walking on socks does not make any noise,' she said. He knew.

They reached the end of the corridor, and before entering the shop floor, Ida pointed to him to wait behind her. She tilted her body slowly forwards and carefully looked into the shop. She turned to him and motioned him down on all fours.

'This game is called "nobody-may-see-me",' she said.

Daniel could feel his cheeks flushing as he followed Ida's path, speedily crawling in between the shop's shelves. They had to stop every time they reached the end of an aisle to see whether the next path was clear. Crawling on it, the shop's floor space seemed gigantic.

'Here comes the trickiest bit.'

Ida had stopped at the end of the bakery shelf. She took out what looked like a bent nail file from underneath the bottom shelf, from there, where the hoover cannot get to. In between them and the fish counter was a scary two-metre gap of open space. Ida listened out, locating her parents by their sounds. Maggie was audibly sipping on an orange juice, something she only did when sitting at her husband's desk, having a break and flicking through a magazine. Koca was outside the shop's front door, whistling while folding the unused carton boxes.

Ida smiled, before she darted to the counter and used the nail file to flick open the cupboard underneath the counter like a door.

And then they were inside the cave.

The empty cupboard was so low that one could only just sit in it. Daniel had to arch his back. One side of the cupboard, the one they came in on, had two peepholes in it. Looking through, it gave an astonishingly good view of the shop, right up to the till. The other side of the cupboard faced towards the back of the counter. There was no wooden wall on this side; instead they were hidden behind fabric attached to a string, like a curtain. It was just a bit too short to reach the floor.

Through the peephole, he saw Koca's feet approaching the fish counter. He was carrying a white polystyrene box. And then he saw his worn leather shoes appearing and disappearing in the tiny opening underneath the curtain. Koca dumped what he was carrying onto the cupboard, the top of which was his work surface. By the smell and sound of it, he seemed to be handling fish. Daniel breathed as quietly as he could. He couldn't believe that Ida was so careless to let half of her foot dangle out from underneath the curtain.

'He could have seen your foot!' Daniel whispered, as soon as Koca had gone again.

'Oops,' she whispered back, 'that happens all the time!' She shuffled her foot inside the cupboard.

'I don't understand,' he said, 'I'm sure Koca must have noticed your hiding place before?'

'Well, it's only a *game*. It's not *real*.' She rolled her eyes as she said 'real' in an overly pronounced way, like 'reeaalll'.

'What's the point of all the sneaking, then? Why did we

have to be so careful?' not bothering to whisper anymore.

'Pssst!'

She looked at him crossly. 'Because it's the rules of the game. Nobody is allowed to see you. Or hear you, for that matter.'

'What a stupid game,' he said.

'You don't have to play,' she whispered. 'I thought you liked sneaking.'

Did she look upset? It was the first time he'd seen her without the confident smile in her eyes. Sitting in this confined space with that girl, he didn't know how to react. He could not just climb out of the cupboard. It would look so ridiculous. Even if the Kocas knew about her silly game.

But he also felt strangely compelled not to break the rules. He knew all about making up games and rules. Only his games were a bit more real than hers. They were serious experiments.

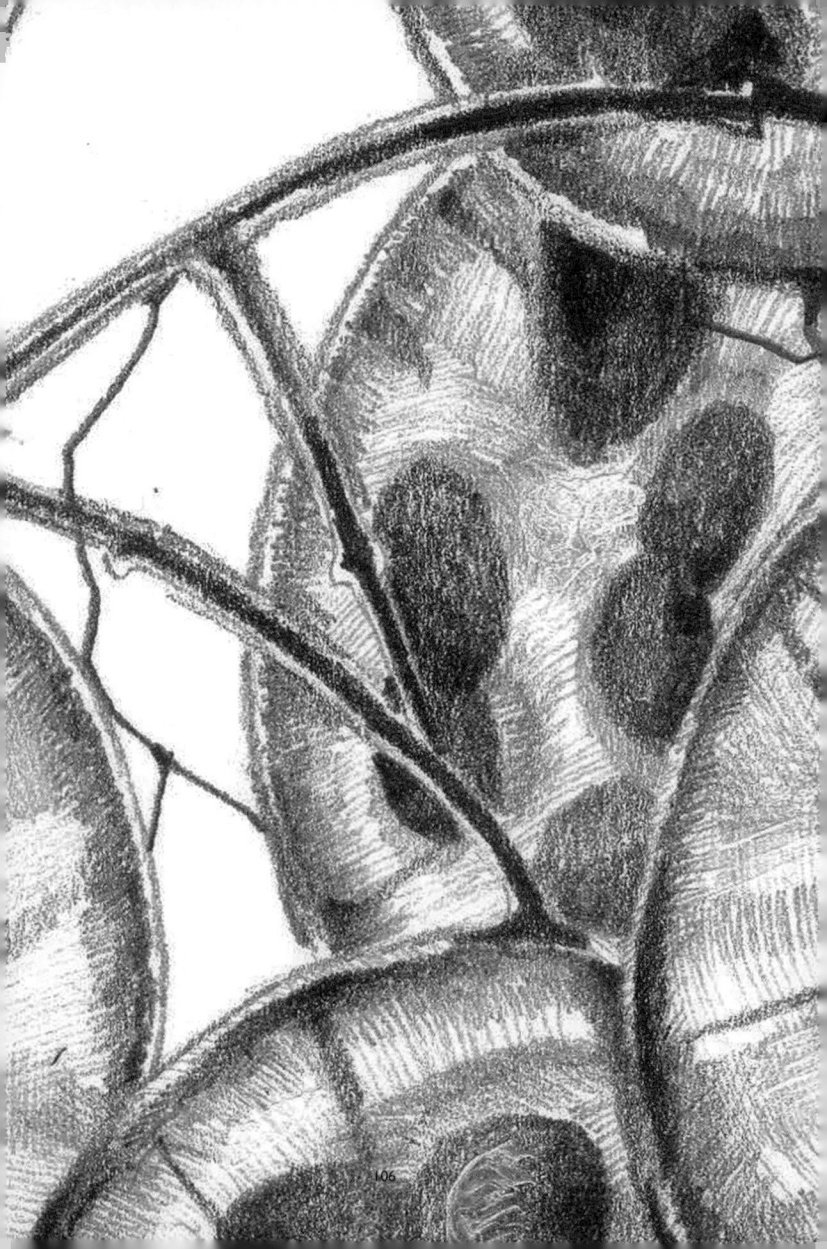

POETRY

Margaret Lewis
Things I Learnt in July

That an oak eggar moth, furry in the sun, can hang all day on a dark grass stalk
That mica sparkles in heather edged granite
That folded hollows can hide dark pools
That curlew cries sound desolate
That sun shivers creep despite the heat
That ghosts linger in the grain of the land
That emigrants sometimes return
That intense pressure's shock creates microdiamonds in limestone
That the margin is thin between control and its loss
That despair seeps up through chinks in the floor
That dead rats bloat
That cars can float
That towns are built on sewage and mud
That vermin filches what it can
That water leaves tidemarks on lives
That community can cross oceans
That childhood light lasts a lifetime
That sun warmed granite can comfort
That a hovering kestrel, seen from above, is reddish brown with black-tipped wings
That distressed trees whisper secrets
That hidden wounds weep into muscle and bone
That shocked quartz bears witness to disaster
That emigrants sometimes come home

SHORT STORY

Lorna Festa
Déjà Vous

The sun woke me only moments ago. I was lying in bed, but now I pass into my bathroom. My toothbrush glides across my teeth, as I avoid my face in the mirror and instead, glare at the sun. Neglecting most of my molars, I rinse off the brush, spit into my towel, and leave the bathroom.

I want to eat Cream of Wheat for breakfast, but I don't have any. This is not my mother's house. The cupboards here are bare. I melt from merely looking outside. I will not go to the river or through town. I won't meet my friends there today. A picture of my former teeth-brushing companion rests on my dresser. He stares at me from his three-by-seven frame. I suffocate the image, turning it face down on itself.

I take myself for a walk. I do not bring a leash.

Trees create a lace canopy as they hang their heavy heads conjuring all ambiance and no protection from the sun. Rays of light push limbs like arms, hands, fingers, ahead of my deliberate stride. My own shadow appears like another person moving past me.

Waiting for me beyond hanging Spanish moss, my mother kneels in the grass, planting impatiens. I lean over her, watching her hands stir up dust from the parched soil. Without a word, she finishes patting down the dirt over the web of roots and lifts herself. She is muddling over something while she removes one of her gardening gloves to untangle her hair. You haven't come up to visit in a while, she says. Your father misses you, she says.

I fumble through my purse and extract a cigarette. Placing the filter between two sticky lips, I continue my aimless stroll. My mother follows several paces behind. I can hear her nagging sneakers shuffling on the road. My cigarette droops unlit from my teeth.

I decide to light it after spotting another familiar figure in the distance. I don't know why I chose the route past Gabriel's house. He slouches over his mailbox, reaching inside, grasping only air. His disappointed eyes flash at me as I flick the lighter on, then off. His expression now is different from the one in the picture. He ignores my mother and saunters along beside me, leaving the mailbox hanging open like a yawn.

Why are you avoiding my calls? he hisses. He doesn't tag along like a lost puppy as he used to; he follows me like a child follows an ice cream truck. In pursuit.

Something smells gamey. Ahead, a small squirrel lies lifeless in the road, sizzling on a black asphalt stovetop. There is not much blood, but then again, there is not much squirrel. There are, however, quite a few flies. I look away. I don't like flies. People say they're necessary for decomposition, but dead things decompose anyway. People are always trying to make up reasons why things are useful or important. The truth is, there is not a reason for everything.

Trevor, an old drinking buddy of mine, is jogging towards me and the others. Sweat drips down his face and bare chest. His head bobs as it would when he was getting too drunk, as though he couldn't balance it on his own neck. He slows his pace and from behind my shoulder he reminds me it hasn't slipped his mind that I owe him a drink.

Maybe two, he chuckles eerily. It was an expensive drink.

I continue on in silence. The dead squirrel is still on my mind. I imagine how this little rodent would have zigzagged in front of the car before the moment of impact. I once read somewhere that squirrels do that to confuse predators. It's a defence tactic, one that doesn't work against a car.

Stupid rat, Gabriel says, as though he can read my thoughts.

Today, I take no shortcuts. I am headed the long way home, if I'm even heading home. When I turn the corner, a sense of *déjà vous* or *je ne sais quoi* or something I can only explain in French comes over me. For a moment this street looks identical to the block my elementary school was on. I see the portable classrooms and the main building and the playground. I see a girl sitting in the grass making a whistle with one of the blades. Then, the jungle gym and the school behind her are gone and it's just Stephanie brushing dirt off her dress as she stands. Behind her is a closed down convenience store with the windows busted in. She skips toward me, arms open. You want to go climb trees, she asks me.

The answer is unfortunately the same as the last time she asked me, almost two decades earlier. Today's not a good day.

She stops skipping and she starts dragging her feet. I watch tree limbs dance around her. The sun is beginning to make me feel translucent. Present company included.

Searching for shade, I push open the wrought-iron gate of the cemetery and step inside. There are squirrels running up and down trees in individual frenzies. I wonder if they are upset about their friend; maybe they are planning him a funeral. One squirrel freezes in place and blinks at me. He thinks I can't see him.

I weave in between stones because the grass is overgrown and there is no path. My grandfather hovers over me beaming. I am shocked and almost fall backwards, but I correct myself and look into his gruff smiling face. My eyes fill with big grown up tears.

What's wrong, doll-face, he says.

The sun is beaming behind him, and I look away. He scratches his beard the way he used to when something was troubling him. He laughs.

Is this about that boy Gabriel? I say you give him the boot.

I want to tell him he's allowed to let go, but I've told him that once before.

There is another man up ahead, and I cringe to think who awaits me still. Lighting another cigarette, I inhale so deeply the smoke makes me cough a little. I feel lightheaded from the heat, but I don't sit down. The others mumble and sigh behind me.

When I reach the man, I see he is homeless. He is not like the others. I don't know this man. He is sitting under an awning with about five tied-up grocery bags to both sides of him. He requests a cigarette, and I hand him one.

You shouldn't talk to strangers, Stephanie says.

This is why I worry about you, Gabriel says.

Don't give him any money, my mom says. He'll just spend it on drugs.

Ask him if he does any tricks, Trevor says.

Keep walking, my grampa says.

A squirrel scampers up a tree. The sun scorches the ground I'm standing on. My feet burn a little through my sneakers.

Thank ya, the homeless man says, tipping his World's Best Dad cap to me. I really needed one 'a these. You're not lookin' too good yerself.

I shrug, and start to walk away.

Just looks like you have a mob after you, he calls to me. Good luck with 'em.

I stop, and turn back around.

You can see them?

He scratches his head. See who? All's I was sayin' is, it

looks like you seen a ghost, is all.

I shake my head and leave him under the awning. When I reach the gate at the other side, I open it, and step out, once again into full sunlight. I close my eyes. I can hear them. They follow me even still. When I was in college, I used to have panic attacks if there were too many people in the room. My therapist told me it was a by-product of obsessive-compulsive disorder. He recommended that I make up a 'ceremonial procedure' to calm myself down.

I used to close my eyes, and picture everyone in the room. Then I would count the number of eyes in the room, person by person. Next, I would multiply that number by five (to get the number of fingers in the room) and then I'd count backwards by that number. As I counted, I would breathe slowly, and the imagined people would disappear. When I opened my eyes again, of course, they were still there, but my heart would no longer be racing.

I close my eyes and count: one two three four five six seven eight nine ten. Then I multiply, and get fifty. Then I breathe, and breathe, and breathe.

When I open my eyes their voices are hushed, and I keep walking. I am cutting through an open field, going home. The sun is brighter than ever, and sweat drips off my nose and makes my clothes stick to my skin.

There is no shade here. Not one damn tree.

Matter is (and always was) a stylish, grown-up, proper magazine ... because it looks so good, because established writers are published alongside student writers ... being published in Matter is a big deal and a pleasure.
Tony Williams

Matter has been a journey, of new friends and new places. Trips to Hay on Wye, to London, a mention in 'Time Out.' ... trawling the bookshops with copies to sell, selling copies at the launch – me and Em getting drunk on the free red wine – good fun, good writing.
Bryony Doran

The MA Writing at Sheffield Hallam University was a turning point for me ... it gave me the space and encouragement to develop as a writer ... Matter introduces you to the work of some of tomorrow's best writers before they get famous ... There is something very exciting about the virtuosity and freshness of undiscovered talent, and this is amply evident in this wonderful collection of poetry and prose ...
Marina Lewycka

... a designated and beautifully-designed space where new writing stands up beside the big names ... my fondest memories of Matter aren't from appearing in it, but from editing an issue with a group of close friends in 2006. Lots of food, lots of arguments. It taught me as much as any seminar did about taste and judgement, not to mention publishing.
Frances Leviston

The artistic quality of the content is matched by fresh design and production values making Matter a very sexy product. It was a real privilege to be involved in several issues of Matter, as both a contributor and poetry editor.
Cathy Bolton

Matter's success stems from having carved out its own unique territory. Always stylishly produced; edited by a changing student board; committed to publishing the very best work from both Hallam's MA Writing and the most exciting established authors around … it's a magazine like no other, that holds its own with the best.
Ben Wilkinson

Matter is a way of gathering the best of writing in all genres, and getting a real feel for the range of talent on the course ... The quality of Matter is the result of the wide range of experience that people bring to the writing at Sheffield, and to the Matter production team.
Anna Chilvers

From the beginning, Matter was an ambitious and therefore a beautiful little magazine. It really counts if your work appears in its pages (painfully, I've been turned down and deliriously, have been accepted)
 ... universities at their best harness the illogical and boundless intensity, hard work and love of those who work and study in English Departments and Creative Writing Programs and from them, can come something like Matter. And ten years of love and good writing. Happy Birthday, Matter.
Gabeba Baderoon

Contributors

Angelina Ayers
Angelina Ayers is editor of *Matter 10*, and was poetry editor of *Matter 9*. She also edited *Best of MA Writing 2009*. Angelina has poems published in *The North*, *Matter* and *Frogmore Papers*. She was short-listed for the 2009 Sheffield Poetry Prize, and is writer in residence at Bank Street Arts.

Rosemary Badcoe
Rosemary Badcoe began the MA Writing in 2010. She has been writing for a number of years and is keen to explore the joins between science and poetry, and the links back to the Anglo-Saxon. She also writes for children and has some science poems soon to be published in an anthology by A&C Black.

Tanya Chan-Sam
Tanya Chan-Sam lives in Cape Town, South Africa. Her writing is published in anthologies and journals in South Africa and the UK. She has given readings at literary festivals, street theatre festivals, schools and universities in the UK, USA and South Africa. Her storytelling has been called elegant, uncommon and exceptional, (Scholars without Borders, 2009; Unheard Words, 2008). *Mr Mohani and Other Stories* (Peepal Tree Press, 2008) is her preview collection of short stories.

Jamie Coward
Jamie Coward is 38 and lives in Sheffield. He's a copywriter in the University of Sheffield's marketing team and a part-time student on the MA Writing.

Margaret Drabble
Margaret Drabble was born in Sheffield in 1939, and has published 17 novels, most recently *The Sea Lady* (Penguin 2008). Her memoir, *The Pattern in the Carpet* (Atlantic), was published in 2009. She is married to the biographer Michael Holroyd.

Tricia Durdey
Tricia Durdey lives in Derbyshire with her husband, son, and a retired racing greyhound. She dances, writes, and teaches Pilates. She has had short stories published by *Mslexia* and Cinnamon Press, amongst others.

Suzannah Evans
Suzannah Evans grew up in Worcestershire and now lives in Leeds. She started the MA at Hallam in October 2009. She has had poems published in a few magazines including *The Rialto* and *Brittle Star*. She is also a poetry editor for *Cadaverine*, an online magazine for under-25s. The rest of the time she works as a debt counsellor.

Lorna Festa

Lorna Festa is a 24-year-old US native. After earning a BA in Psychology with honours and working as an advertisement scriptwriter, she decided to move to Sheffield. She is currently writing an existential coming-of-age novel, Killer & the Crooks, which was selected for the Best of MA Writing at Sheffield Hallam. She believes that experience is the greatest method for research. When she is not writing, Lorna enjoys cycling and lurking in cafes and pubs.

Diana Gabaldon

Diana Gabaldon is the author of the award-winning, #1 New York Times-bestselling *OUTLANDER* novels, described by *Salon* magazine as 'the smartest historical sci-fi adventure-romance story ever written by a science Ph.D. with a background in scripting "Scrooge McDuck" comics.'
19 million copies are in print in 26 countries and 22 languages.

Margaret Lewis

After a lifetime of procrastination – merely postponing the inevitable – Margaret Lewis is now giving herself time (and permission) to write. Her true home is in the hills, but she lives in Sheffield and edits a magazine for long distance cyclists.

Dean Lilleyman

Dean Lilleyman studied for a degree in Film and Literature at Sheffield Hallam. He graduated in 2008 winning the Percy Snowden Writing Prize. He is currently on the MA Writing course as recipient of the Archie Markham Scholarship. He is working on a novel called *Billy and the Devil*.

Fay Musselwhite

Fay Musselwhite moved to Sheffield from the south coast in the late '90s and likes it. Her poetry has been placed in competitions, and published in magazines, including *Cake* and *The North*. Fay is fascinated by the river Rivelin, which flows from the Peak District to near her home and has an industrial past; her work is frequently set there.

Daljit Nagra

Daljit Nagra comes from a Punjabi background. In 2004 he won the Forward Prize for Best Individual Poem with 'Look We Have Coming to Dover!' This was the title of his first collection, published by Faber & Faber in 2007, which won the Forward Prize for Best First Collection and The South Bank Show Decibel Award. Daljit is on the Board of the Poetry Book Society. He has judged several competitions including The National Poetry Competition 2009. He also hosted the TS Eliot Poetry Readings 2009.

Kate Rutter

Kate Rutter lives in Sheffield. She trained as an actor at Rose Bruford College and has worked extensively in theatre, film, television and radio. She has written drama for the stage throughout her career and is currently concentrating on poetry and prose. She was a prizewinner in The Mirehouse Poetry Competition judged by Ruth Padel.

Iain Sinclair

Iain Sinclair has lived in Hackney since 1969. His books include *Downriver, Dining on Stones, Lights out for the Territory, London Orbital* and *Edge of the Orison*. He edited *London: City of Disappearances* in October 2006. His most recent publication is *Hackney, That Rose Red Empire* (February 2009).

Arto Vaun

Originally from Boston, Arto Vaun's first book, Capillarity, was published by Carcanet Press (2009). One of the poems was selected for the 2010 Forward Book of Poetry.
He is working on a second collection while completing a PhD in Creative Writing at Glasgow University. He is also a songwriter, performing as Mishima USA, Tsui, and The Kent 100s.

Elisabeth Von Aster

Lisi Von Aster had never heard of Sheffield before; now she finds that she s been living here the past two years. It is different from Berlin, her hometown, and Zurich, her other hometown. But she likes it and will stay. Most importantly, it has made her start writing a novel.

Laura Wake

Laura Wake worked as a ski instructor before deciding to do an English degree in 2005. She was awarded the Percy Snowden prize for writing in her final year and chose to do the MA Writing course. She is working on her first novel, and also writes short stories and scripts.

Noel Williams

Noel Williams is a Resident Poet at Sheffield's Bank Street Arts Centre, and also works for Art in the Park. Whilst on the MA, he's published 100 poems and won several prizes. Now working towards a collection, his prose is on its way, too. See http://noelwilliams.wordpress.com/

Tudor Players

No! No! No! - Tudor Players is a modern drama group for the 21st century. We are one of the leading amateur drama groups in Sheffield, performing at the Library Theatre adjacent to the Lyceum and Crucible Theatres.

On stage in February, May and October our best productions incude Dad's Army, Brassed Off, 'Allo 'Allo, Amadeus; more recently Darling Buds of May, Flint Street Nativity; coming soon The Dresser, A Servant to two Masters, Calendar Girls.

If acting, directing or watching good theatre is what you enjoy, then visit our website
www.tudorplayers.net

THE 2010 POETRY BUSINESS BOOK & PAMPHLET COMPETITION &

SHEFFIELD POETRY PRIZE
for entrants with a Sheffield post code

JUDGE: Simon Armitage

DEADLINE: last posting on Monday 29th November 2010 (or for online entries, 1st December)

ENTRY FEE: £25 — or £20 for Friends and subscribers. £1 surcharge is applied to entries submitted online

Entrants are invited to submit a short collection of poems (20-24 pages), for the chance to win:

- book publication & six free copies (for the overall winner),
- pamphlet publication & 20 free copies (for three first-stage winners),
- a share of **£2,000** prize money,

And entrants with a Sheffield postcode are automatically entered into the Sheffield Poetry Prize category for the chance to win £100 and publication in The North magazine and on the Poetry Business website.
See **www.poetrybusiness.co.uk** for full details and an entry form (or to enter online).

The University Of Sheffield.

Faculty Of Arts & Humanities.

The Sheffield Poetry Prize category is sponsored by The University of Sheffield.

PURSUE YOUR PASSION
MA WRITING

We have been helping writers to get published since 1993.
We pride ourselves on being one of the few universities offering a writing MA which supervises you through to the completion of a novel, script, or collection of poems or stories. This gives you a great advantage when you step out into the professional world.

We treat your ambition seriously, while offering you the flexibility to study around your existing work or family commitments.

A taste of the course
Do you want to push your writing further but are not in a position to commit to a full MA? If so you can apply to take a single module from the course in one of several genres.

Win a place on the course
Make an application for the January 2011 intake of this course before 1st November 2010 and your short story could win The Archie Markham scholarship, which waives the fees for the course.

For more details visit
www.shu.ac.uk/courses/137

SHARPENS YOUR THINKING

Eleven, the designers of Matter 10, are a graphic design consultancy, working for public and private sector clients creating individual and relevant design solutions. We produce print and online graphics for branding, exhibition, marketing, press and events.

Eleven Design
Globe Works
Penistone Road
S6 3AE
T: 0114 2218120